Press Upwards

Ashley Walmsley

Ark House Press
arkhousepress.com

© 2024 Ashley Walmsley

All rights reserved. Apart from any fair dealing for the purpose of study, research, criticism, or review, as permitted under the Copyright Act, no part may be reproduced by any process without written permission.

Scripture quotations are from The ESV® Bible (The Holy Bible, English Standard Version®), © 2001 by Crossway, a publishing ministry of Good News Publishers. Used by permission. All rights reserved.

Cataloguing in Publication Data:
Title: Press Upwards
ISBN: 978-1-7636468-1-0 (pbk)
Subjects: REL006700   RELIGION / Biblical Studies / Bible Study Guides; REL012020   RELIGION / Christian Living / Devotional; REL109030   RELIGION / Christian Ministry / Youth;

Design by initiateagency.com

INTRODUCTION

What's this all about?

BIBLICAL devotions based on video and computer games- you're kidding, right?

Do Christians even play video games?

Well, yes; yes they do. Just as they eat hamburgers and ride motorcycles and vote in elections and do scrapbooking and run marathons.

The video game industry is mammoth. It continues to grow, pushed on by the interest in mobile gaming and the continual release of updated systems, and even entirely new systems.

It is a mission field like any other, one that exists both online and in reality.

Gamers need to hear the gospel as much as anyone.

The apostle Paul describes how he aimed to communicate the Gospel to people where they were, how he "became like a Jew to win the Jews". (1 Corinthians 9:19-23)

It's hoped this book will do just that.

Video and computer games are instant conversation starters, not just with the youth of today but with almost all ages.

From the retired lady tapping away at *Candy Crush*, to the teenage boy mashing his keyboard over *Minecraft*, or even the mother waiting in the car outside the school amusing herself with *Solitaire*; games are part of modern life.

For those that already know that God loves them, this book aims to uplift, inspire, spark a memory, prompt discussion and maybe even provide a laugh.

For those yet to embrace all that God has for them, it's about stirring a thought, asking more questions, pricking a conscience and tapping a need to know more.

Feel free to share these devotions through whatever means you like.

Perhaps they'll stimulate a conversation at Youth Group; maybe form the basis of a talk at a camp; open up some shared ground at a Bible study; possibly create some debate in the work lunch room or school yard; even trigger some talk at the home dinner table.

So play on, pray on and in the Word, stay on.

WHY THESE GAMES?

SELFISHLY, these are largely games I've played and enjoyed.
But the selection is based on more than that.

These games are within a realm I would classify as "Christian accessibility".

Some might also label them as harmless. (Although *Metal Gear Solid* and *Fortnite* would be the obvious eyebrow raising exceptions to this rule.)

They are relatively tame most of them but as the sales of each would attest, they can also be immensely fun.

The argument over whether Christians should be playing video games in the first place is one that won't be argued here.

Clearly, Christians do play them, just as many watch movies, go to football games, occasionally miss church and binge on chocolate.

In order to have a better idea of the context of each devotional, I'd encourage you to experience the games if you can.

Now, before you or your parents write a letter to me about spending $1000 on this list of software, may I suggest an alternative: YouTube.

There is footage of all of these games on the internet, somewhere. You don't have to watch or play every level, just enough to get a sense of what it's about.

Versions of some of them may even be free to download onto phones, or could be played in browsers.

There is enjoyment in playing a game you may never have before or one that you haven't in a long time.

It may even, dare I suggest it, make a Bible study or devotional time fun.

There are so many games out there, just as there are so many fantastic passages and themes within the Bible that could be explored, dissected and appreciated.

So grab that Bible (or open the app as the case may be), plug in that controller and set your mind to "think".

If you're ready to get closer to God through gaming, press start…

The Gamer's Prayer

Lord God, creator of all things,

We commit this time of gaming to you.

You give us the ability to interact with this technology, and we thank You for that, as we do for creating the machines in the first place.

As we plunge into this digital world, we would ask that You protect our hearts and minds against influences and actions that may go against Your will.

May we be ever aware of Your great and marvellous real world that surrounds us.

Help us Lord, to love those whom we play with and against, knowing we are all Your children.

Keep us level-headed and remind us that even in the heat of competition, whether we are winning or losing, that it is just a game, and You love us despite ranking or achievements.

In Jesus name we pray,

Amen.

INDEX

- Age of Empires 8
- Alex Kidd in Miracle World 10
- Angry Birds 12
- Assassin's Creed 14
- Candy Crush Saga 16
- Daytona USA 18
- Donkey Kong 20
- Farming Simulator 22
- FIFA 24
- Final Fantasy 26
- Fortnite 28
- Frogger 30
- Fruit Ninja 32
- Galaga 34
- Golden Axe 36
- Gran Turismo 38
- Guitar Hero 40
- Kirby's Adventure 42
- Lemmings 44
- Little Big Planet 46
- Mario Kart 49
- Metal Gear Solid 51
- Metroid 53
- Minecraft 55
- Minesweeper 57
- Myst 60
- PAC-Man 62
- Pitfall! 64

- Plants vs Zombies 66
- Pokemon 68
- Pokemon Go 70
- Pong 72
- Portal and Portal 2 74
- Prince of Persia 76
- Punch Out! 78
- R-Type 80
- Sega Rally Championship 82
- SingStar 84
- Snake/Snake II 86
- Solitaire 88
- Sonic the Hedgehog 90
- Street Fighter II 92
- Super Mario Bros. 94
- Tetris 96
- The Legend of Zelda 98
- The Secret of Monkey Island 100
- The Sims 102
- Tomb Raider 104
- Wii Sports 106
- Wonder Boy III: The Dragon's Trap 108

Title: **A View From The Creator's Keyboard**
Game: ***Age of Empires***
Themes: **Love, sacrifice**

THOSE men are mostly obedient when set about a task.

They gather wood or gold or stone like their lives depend on it. Actually, their lives *do* depend on it.

The length of a game of *Age of Empires* is perhaps the briefest of insights into God's perspective.

He'd be a much better player than any of us of course but it's interesting to be immersed in a game where you have complete control over the destiny of the tribe you have created.

Or so it seems.

You might have the armoury built up and the priests all ready to convert people… and then you hear that dreaded trumpet.

What's worse is if you hear the trumpet but can't see the enemy attack.

Panic can set in as you wonder what's happening to one of your little digital family.

Even though you are dishing out the tasks, the unexpected can come at you.

All of a sudden, things have spiraled out of control and smoke is billowing out of your defense tower and an enemy army has annoyingly got a large battle elephant at your doorstep.

Things don't look good.

The easy answer is to pause, quit and start all over. No fuss, no hassle.

God didn't do that. Imagine if He'd finished creating the world we exist in, and then started over when man turned things sour.

He seemed to come close to hitting the reset switch with Noah and the flood but still He didn't give up on His creation.

Why is that? The answer is easy: love. He loved us so much that He was willing to weave salvation into the overall fabric of humanity's story.

Would you be able to do that within a game? Stick with a tribe? But not only the tribe you're focussed on; the opposition armies as well?

He loves all of humanity so much He sent Jesus into the world to save it, to show His ultimate love.

That's like you, as the player, being transported into the game as one of the digital tribe members, sent in to make a difference. Could you, would you do it?

What a tremendous act of courage and bravery and love.

On top of all that is the grace to be able to do that. You'd hardly take instructions from one of the little people in the game if they turned around and said: "Hey, you're doing it all wrong. This is how it should go."

You know a bigger and better plan for your tribe. God knows a bigger and better plan for His people, yet He cares for and listens to each request.

When the Creator becomes part of His creation in order to save it; that's genuine love.

> *"For God so loved the world, that he gave his only Son, that whoever believes in him should not perish but have eternal life."*
>
> *—John 3: 16*

See also… Hebrews 2:17; Romans 5: 6-8; Philippians 2:8

Title: **The Right Documentation**
Game: **Alex Kidd in Miracle World**
Themes: **Jesus as our intercessor**

ALEX Kidd in Miracle World was the game built-in to the Sega Master System II, which meant you could get right into the action as soon as it was out of the box.

Alex (whose last name is apparently "Kidd" despite often wrongly being referred to as "Alex the Kid") is a prince and needs to save the kingdom from some bad dudes.

In order to do this, he'll need to travel throughout the land with the help of a trusty map, punching his way through boulders and enemies, and using items such as the power bracelet, teleport powder and the all-amazing cane of flight.

Though a pretty straightforward platformer, it's not a walk-in-the-park, with some areas presenting headaches (swum through that underwater spike maze yet?) and repetitive frustration if a jump isn't timed right.

But along the way, there is a complex twist. You have to visit High Stone, the ruler of the Kingdom of Nibana. There's no way around it; you have to meet him.

If you arrive at his throne without the required letter, he bluntly asks you to leave; no excuses, no arguing, no second chances. It's almost a digital portrayal of scenes spelt out in the Bible for those who have ignored God's word and rejected Jesus. In warning followers that they need a saviour, Jesus himself spells out what will happen to those who approach the throne of God, still drenched in their sin. God will say, "depart from me for I never knew you" (Matthew 7:23).

In other words, they don't have the right documentation. The "documentation" in this case is Jesus

If Alex goes to High Stone with the personal letter given to him in an earlier stage, he's welcomed in. Everyone has the same opportunity to "discover Jesus" and take hold of Him. In fact, He's actively seeking people out.

Whether they choose to take hold of Him and His promise of Salvation is up to them.

But there will come a point where every individual will appear before Him. Everyone will have to go through that throne room after they die; there's just no avoiding it.

What happens there will depend on your documentation. Did you accept Jesus's offer of forgiveness and have your name listed in the Lamb's Book of Life?

Or did you think you could go it alone? It would be an immense tragedy to have God tell you to leave from His presence.

In *Alex Kidd in Miracle World*, you find favour not because of what you've done, how much money you have or who you are, but simply because you received something given to you freely.

God accepts you because you have Jesus as your "documentation", as your advocate who died in your place to forgive your sins. It's worth seeking out Jesus before moving to the next stage.

> *"And just as it is appointed for man to die once, and after that comes judgment, so Christ, having been offered once to bear the sins of many, will appear a second time, not to deal with sin but to save those who are eagerly waiting for him."*
>
> *—Hebrews 9:27-28*

See also… Romans 8:34; Acts 4:12; 1 John 2: 1-2; Hebrews 7:25

Title: **Angles of Obedience**
Game: **Angry Birds**
Themes: **Obedience**

YEARS before there was *Angry Birds*, there was a very basic computer game played on a PC in high school libraries. (Quite possibly called, *Gorillas*.)

Students would gather around to watch a small, terribly rendered figure launch a rocket from one side of the screen, over some terrain, with the aim of hitting a gorilla or ape-like creature on the other side.

Lining up a shot meant inputting angles and a thrust percentage.

What those cunning teachers were doing by allowing students to play the game was teaching them about geometry and physics.

Oh, the hours that were put in by fun-seeking students, blissfully unaware they were actually learning.

It was all about trajectory.

Fast forward 30 years and we have the same basic concept but with cute, somewhat overweight birds and perhaps even cuter (and even more overweight) snorting green pigs.

Millions of people, hardcore gamers and casuals alike, enjoy pulling back the slingshot to launch a bird into the towers built by those nasty piggies.

They hope and practise for direct hits on the small green enemy. Sometimes they target the base of a wobbly structure that would certainly not pass local council approval.

Again, it's all about trajectory, providing the same fun as it did back in the school library.

If your aim is off, or if it strays a bit, then chances are it's not going to hit the mark.

Life trajectories can be "off" as well. If we're not aiming for Jesus, setting our sights on Him or if we're taking our eyes off the prize, then it gets worse after we "fire".

We find that a little bit of movement, a bit of sin that's left to fester in our lives, will bump off our angle.

If not lined up correctly, the shot can miss completely or affect something we don't want it to.

Our misdirected actions, those not guided by God, can have consequences for others, like the ricochet effect on the pigs' towers, with knock-on repercussions.

We may not have a dotted guideline that we move around to see where our actions will impact but we've got the Bible that contains all the aiming instructions we need.

God gives us the right trajectory in every situation.

> *"Looking to Jesus, the founder and perfecter of our faith, who for the joy that was set before him endured the cross, despising the shame, and is seated at the right hand of the throne of God."*
>
> *—Hebrews 12:2*

See also… 1 Peter 2: 4-8; Romans 5: 19; Deuteronomy 28: 1

Title: Blending In To Share
Game: Assassin's Creed
Themes: Testimony, witnessing

DO not kill. That's a pretty clear instruction from the Bible, and one that goes against the very idea of the *Assassin's Creed* line of games.

The job of an assassin is to assassinate, to eliminate, to kill.

Despite its non-Christian goal, perhaps we can take something from the lead character in his approach.

Yes he can do some sinister stuff with elaborate moves but a very big part of his approach is blending in, becoming part of the culture of wherever he is.

He doesn't give in to all the temptations around him or succumb to the influence of the townspeople but stealthily moves through like he's meant to be there.

We shouldn't hide our commitment to Christ; No one lights a lamp and puts it in a place where it will be hidden, or under a bowl (Luke 11:33). We are told to be the light and fragrance of Christ so we need to be seen and heard.

We are, however, to be wise on how we interact with the world, with non-Christians.

In Colossians 4: 5-6, Paul gives that very instruction, adding we should make the most of every opportunity with them.

That may mean blending in somewhat, getting to know the people we work, play, commute, shop or holiday with in order to be ready for an opportunity to share the story of Jesus with them. That means being among them, not in a bubble waiting to be asked.

It might not even be a full blown conversation but perhaps a comment here and there, a reference to your church or something you read in the Bible or how God provided for you in a desperate situation. Paul also says your conversation should be gracious and effective so we'll have the right answer for everyone.

It does the assassin no good to speak harshly to all he meets because he'll instantly be labeled an enemy.

Of course, we don't want to soften the message or dilute our testimony by doing something that goes against God's instruction. It's about refining how we deliver the message.

And if it all seems a bit overwhelming being in the same town, situation, travel route, institution or wherever and not having any opportunities for conversations, then another manoeuvre might work; step back. The lead character in *Assassin's Creed* loves to climb to the highest point in the city and peer down. It helps to get a bigger picture perspective.

This isn't advocating you don a 19th century hoodie and shinny up the top of the local church steeple. Rather, by reminding yourself of the bigger picture, that all these people you interact with are God's loved creations that He longs to save, then it may just help to reinvigorate your mission to share the Good News.

Unlike *Assassin's Creed*, we want to deliver life to people, not take it from them. That may just take careful steps and wise moves.

"Walk in wisdom toward outsiders, making the best use of the time."

—*Colossians 4:5*

See also… 1 Peter 3: 15-16, Ephesians 5: 15-17; 1 Peter 3: 15-16

Title: A Crushing Addiction
Game: *Candy Crush Saga*
Themes: Addiction

THERE is a tremendous sense of achievement watching candies vanish with a sparkle.

Just to clarify: that statement is in reference to *Candy Crush Saga*; not wrapping boiled lollies in aluminium foil and sticking them in a microwave.

To see those lines combust with sparkly stars dancing everywhere as you make a three, four, five (or more) in-a-row combination delivers the videogame version of a warm hug every time.

And then it's onto the next line or combination. Then the next, then the next.

That lure, that draw, that temptation to just go one more round; to see if you can reach the next level and what new treats await you there is very strong.

It really does become a saga when time slides past as you stare at those throbbingly bright pixels.

Like many good puzzle games, *Candy Crush Saga* relies on addiction.

Sure, it's not going to give you lung cancer, destroy your liver or max-out your credit card (unless you're really, REALLY into the in-game purchases) like some other addictions, but the repetitive attraction is there.

The thing about addictions is that they can make other parts, and people, in our lives suffer.

There are so many elements that make *Candy Crush Saga* addictive; the ease of play; the colours; and, as mentioned at the start, that sense of accomplishment.

When the phone, tablet or controller is put down or the PC turned off though, what's been accomplished?

Improved hand-eye coordination? Increased brain stimulation? Those unintended bonuses might be there but could something have been done with a family member or friend that could also have improved those areas, as well as connecting and showing God's love to them?

There are plenty of tricks and techniques to master for making those candies disappear and drop. Be sure to master another skill as well; being able to walk away from it when needed.

This goes for all video and computer games. The ability to shut down and move on can be as difficult as perfecting the game itself.

Addictions, whatever they are over, need to be confronted and controlled. With God's help, that's very achievable. Delicious!

"All things are lawful for me," but not all things are helpful. "All things are lawful for me," but I will not be dominated by anything."

—1 Corinthians 6:12

See also… 1 Corinthians 10:13; 1 Peter 5:8; James 1:12-15

Title: Holding Strong on Life's Race Track
Game: *Daytona USA*
Themes: Endurance, resilience

ENDURANCE. Patience. Longsuffering.

They are all qualities the Bible uses to describe living a Christian life.

They are also qualities which come in quite handy when pressing the accelerator flat to the floor in a stock car named Hornet while ripping around the Daytona International Speedway.

Daytona USA, developed by Sega, is widely regarded as one of the most successful arcade games to have ever been created.

For a game released in 1993, it has a remarkably long lifespan, being still found in cinema foyers, bowling alleys and airport arcades around the world.

Players choose from three circuits - beginner (eight laps), advanced (four laps) and expert (two laps).

These tracks aren't just for a leisurely Sunday meander around the block though. They can be hard and taxing, requiring continued concentration from the player.

Egging you on through the game is that throbbing theme music with the catchy line, "Daytonaaaaaaaaaaaa" infiltrating your ears, probably for the rest of the day.

Of course, you're not the only one on the track, so just navigating the corners and straights isn't enough; you have to allow for other players.

Here's where those qualities mentioned at the start - endurance, patience, longsuffering - come into play.

The Apostle Paul likes to use these words in his New Testament letters to churches and individual Christians.

They are used to encourage and inspire the recipient to keep on going, to press on, to not lose heart in this life.

Living God's way is an endurance event. There are other players jostling, bumping (sometimes on purpose) and knocking you about to get ahead, to get in front or just to damage you on purpose.

At these moments, it's vital to keep pushing forward, to absorb the knocks and rumble on. Even if you suffer a major crash (ie. give in to an addiction, have a severe break-up with a friend, lose a colleague/job/title), God doesn't want you to stay there, bogged in anguish.

The Bible says God gives endurance (Romans 15:5) so He fully understands the need to keep going, even if you're taking a few knocks and your tyres are now lumpy.

Feeling a bit like a beaten up stock car after seven laps? Go to God for a pitstop and reset. He'll refresh you, ready for another "rolling staaaaaaaarrrrrttttt!".

> *"Therefore, since we are surrounded by so great a cloud of witnesses, let us also lay aside every weight, and sin which clings so closely, and let us run with endurance the race that is set before us."*
>
> *—Hebrews 12: 1*

See also… 2 Timothy 2: 3; Romans 15: 4-5; Revelation 14: 12; 2 Corinthians 6: 4

Title: **Dropping the Hammer of Power**
Game: ***Donkey Kong***
Themes: **Strength in weakness**

DONKEY Kong sure has had some adventures over the years.

Donkey Kong Country sees him belt along in 3D; he pops up in *Super Smash Bros* and then there is *Donkey Konga*, the game that came with a set of bongo drums on the GameCube, a gimmick that perhaps didn't sell as well as Nintendo had hoped, which is a pity because they could have gone on to release an entire reggae band.

In Donkey Kong's first gaming appearance though, he wasn't even the character the player controlled, despite the game being named after him.

The original arcade version saw a small dude named Jumpman (looking curiously like Mario) on a quest to rescue a lass named Pauline from the chest-beating ape.

Donkey Kong keeps on throwing barrels down the platforms and Jumpman is forced to, well, jump, hastily climb ladders or grab a hammer to destroy the barrels.

Ahh yes, the hammer- what a feeling of power for a few seconds.

It allows you to smash the barrels as they fall, not only getting them out of the road but giving you extra points to boot.

Here's the thing though; you'll never finish the game with the hammer in your hand. It may seem like the ultimate weapon on *Donkey Kong* but it's actually a limiting factor.

Power trips don't last in life either. In fact, whatever our "hammer" is (a position, money, a piece of information, an ability, etc), it can provide a false sense of security, holding us back from becoming what God truly wants of us.

You can't climb a ladder while holding the hammer in *Donkey Kong*; you've got to get rid of it to move on.

In our Christian lives, we need to let go of things that make us feel powerful, make us think we are the ones with the force to change the world, or replace our need for God in our lives.

Only God has the power to truly make a difference in a person's life. He uses us most effectively when we've given up everything, when we don't feel powerful, when we don't have the barrel-bashing hammer in our hands.

Think Jonah inside a fish's stomach; think Moses out in the middle of a desert; think Paul when he's in prison, been shipwrecked, bitten by a snake and tortured.

This allows others to see God's might working through us as vessels. Imagine if someone said the only reason you beat *Donkey Kong* was because of the hammer. You'd feel annoyed because it takes so much more than that.

Don't get stuck on a pink girder of life, holding onto a hammer you believe makes you powerful.

Chances are it's not going to last forever and it'll hold you back from being who God wants you to be.

Becoming vulnerable might seem scary but that's when God can use us the most. When we let go of it, He'll grab onto us.

"For the sake of Christ, then, I am content with weaknesses, insults, hardships, persecutions, and calamities. For when I am weak, then I am strong."

—2 Corinthians 12: 10

See also… 2 Corinthians 12: 9; Romans 8:26; 2 Corinthians 10:17

Title: **Harvesting Consequences**
Game: *Farming Simulator*
Themes: **Consequences**

THERE is an excitement to being reckless.

It's not what you might expect from a game based on agriculture but here is a world where actions don't seem to have consequences.

For instance, there is joy to be had in driving a shiny, expensive tractor into a water reservoir to see what happens.

(It sinks to the bottom and stays there while the player is magically "transferred" out of the vehicle onto dry land.)

The machines can be reset, which means they appear back on the farm as if they'd never left.

Other adventures can be had by driving a grain harvester full pelt at an oncoming car, or seeing what angle a tractor towing a water tank can be driven at along a rocky outcrop before it tips and rolls to the bottom.

It's not like modern racing games where the car sustains damage and costs the user. In *Farming Simulator*, you just keep on ploughing on - literally.

Doing these kinds of acts in real life would not only be dangerous but would most likely cost a person a lot of money, not to mention broken parts of his or her body.

In the context of a game, you can get away with just about anything. That's the beauty of video and computer games in general; they allow you to experience and do things you wouldn't otherwise do.

Real life has consequences though.

Decisions and actions affect ourselves and other people, whether we like or anticipate it, or not.

It's human nature to consider how a certain course of action will affect ourselves.

Our communities would be better off if we considered how the particular decision we are about to make is going to affect our neighbour, parents, guardians, relatives, co-workers, employer, etc.

Making decisions with the good of others in mind is a more Godly way of thinking.

There can be a temporary excitement to reckless decisions in life. Sure, we might not drive a livestock trailer into a lake for a laugh but the temptation is there for instant thrills and cheap gratification, regardless of how it might impact another human.

When it comes to decisions, it should really boil down to asking two things:

1) Will this bring glory to God?
2) Am I showing love to others by doing this?

And don't use your tractor as a submarine.

> *"And you shall love the Lord your God with all your heart and with all your soul and with all your mind and with all your strength.' The second is this: 'You shall love your neighbor as yourself.' There is no other commandment greater than these."*
>
> *—Mark 12: 30-31*

See also… Galatians 6:7; Proverbs 25:26

Title: **The Power Switch**
Game: *FIFA*
Themes: **Authority**

PLAYING soccer (or football, as it's referred to in some parts) in real life is vastly different to playing it with a controller in your hand.

FIFA _____ (insert whatever particular year in that space), by Electronic Arts (EA) continues to dominate the landscape of soccer games on various platforms.

Games involving sports teams must be difficult to program because unlike baseball or cricket in which sides take turns, team sports are continuous and gameplay relies on players being able to switch between offense and defense each time ball possession changes.

When it does, the controls change. The kick button becomes a tackle and the pass becomes a jostle, or whatever.

What is actually switching is control, or power.

It's a good feeling to be charging down the field with the ball at your feet, putting on a burst of speed, doing a few tricks, then missiling it towards the goal box.

It's a different story when the opposition is tearing away with the ball and you're floundering to get back in time, frantically switching between players hoping to take control of the one nearest the ball in order to steal it or at least get in the other team's way.

It's easy to feel in control when we have power; when we are captain of the team; the oldest in the group; the biggest on the field; know the most about a project; or are the boss.

Our attitude, like the game controls, tends to change when the soccer boot is on the other foot and we have to take orders or do as instructed.

Jesus was both the most powerful person on earth and yet the most humble. He knew how to serve and be served. We are to respect the authority of those who have it. They've been put into their position for a purpose, perhaps one they can't even see.

We need to be sure we don't undermine or aim to make their life tougher than it already is.

On the other hand, there will probably come a time when we are in charge of someone or something, or even a group of someones or somethings.

In the *FIFA* games particularly, it's a temporary power shift. Sometimes it can switch rapidly in a matter of seconds.

God may grant and strip power as swiftly as that. It happened to various kings and rulers in the Bible.

Don't get attached to where you are. If you're at the top, be mindful it may not be forever.

If you're keeping your head down as a willing worker, know that at some point you may have to rise up in order to serve a bigger purpose and share the load.

The next time you're mashing away at the control pad or keyboard trying to get your team over the line or the ball in the back of the net or in the basket, keep in mind how the control of power switches. Remember; God, "the ultimate boss", always has final control.

"Let every person be subject to the governing authorities. For there is no authority except from God, and those that exist have been instituted by God."

—*Romans 13: 1*

See also… 1 Peter 2: 13; Romans 13: 2; Hebrews 13:17

Title: **Prior Knowledge Not Required**
Game: *Final Fantasy*
Themes: **Reading the Bible**

AN attempt to conquer all the *Final Fantasy* games in order is an ambitious quest, perhaps more ambitious than one of the storylines of the games themselves. It would take hundreds of hours to plough through, from the original 1987 installment to whatever it is currently up to by the time this is published.

The series has a longevity that few others do.

You might think that by playing *Final Fantasy VII* (that's "seven" for those not from Rome) or *Final Fantasy X* without playing games I-VI would throw you in completely unprepared for what's to come but that's not the case.

As extensive as the series is, each game is pretty much a stand alone adventure.

There's no need to have played every previous title in order to jump into *Final Fantasy XVI* for instance.

The idea of turn-based battle, swords, magic and an other-worldy realm that needs saving could be considered basic building blocks for each game.

Those that have a history of playing them will find a deeper richness from them however, noting the references to returning characters or "in jokes" (ridden a Chocobo lately?).

Asking someone to pick up a Bible who has never done so in their life could present similar feelings to picking up a controller and staring down the entire *Final Fantasy* series.

It's a big book, full of individual, seemingly standalone stories of vastly different storylines.

But you don't have to have read it from front to back in order to find the treasures within and be changed by it.

It can be picked up and opened at any point of the 66 books within and the reader can be assured it is God's word, no matter how seemingly strange or poetic or raw it might be.

And it will have an impact on the reader, whether they acknowledge it or not; it has the power to cut into the thoughts and penetrate to the soul of the reader (Hebrews 4:12) like one of the many two-edged swords swung by *Final Fantasy* characters.

Like returning *Final Fantasy* players, returning readers will get a deeper richness from the Bible over time. They will see the connections, the references to characters past, the prophetic fulfilments in the New Testament of things spoken about in the Old Testament.

The difference between *Final Fantasy* and the Bible of course, is that there *is* has an overarching theme: it is the story of Jesus (Luke 24:25-27).

The story of His love for the world is there in each book, even if not immediately evident.

Don't be intimidated or overwhelmed by the concept of reading the Bible or encouraging others to do so. God has given it to the world to digest, to inspire, to encourage, to discern, to learn from, to correct us and to convict. Just jump right in. That's what Cid would tell you to do.

"All Scripture is breathed out by God and profitable for teaching, for reproof, for correction, and for training in righteousness, that the man of God may be complete, equipped for every good work."

—2 Timothy 3:16–17

See also… Hebrews 4:12; Psalm 12:6; Proverbs 3:5-6; Jeremiah 23:29

Title: **Purple Doom Cometh**
Game: *Fortnite*
Themes: **Death, eternal life**

YOU can't outrun the storm.

No matter how quick your player is, no matter how many grapplers, grappling gloves, or Movement Modulators, rare spicy fish or peppers you get your hands on, that big purple haze keeps on moving in. And it's not like it comes as a surprise either. The game alerts you from the start that a storm is coming. It then becomes a decision of what to do at that point.

Sure, the point of *Fortnite* is to survive, which essentially means gunning down every other player. But sometimes, depending on where you drop-in on the map, it can seem like you're the only one on the planet.

Interactions with other avatars can be sporadic which seems to be a good thing, allowing you time to gear up with weapons, resources, perhaps even build a base.

But the clock keeps ticking and that storm keeps coming.

Taxes and death are traditionally trotted out as the two unavoidable things in life.

While some clever bookwork by shady accountants employed by billionaires may avoid the question of taxes, death, however, is unavoidable.

It's coming, looming, zoning in at every moment. Every day you live is another day closer to the day you die.

That may be a pretty grim thought for many who've never taken the time to consider it.

We can spend a fair amount of our time gearing up in life; trying to get the best education or live out the most exciting experiences, perhaps working to secure that ideal job or just collect every "toy" we possibly can.

Meanwhile, the aubergine shadow (perhaps not technically aubergine) creeps closer and closer.

Like the *Fortnite* warnings, the Bible gives plenty of warning that it is inevitable. Death is a consequence of man's sin, something we all have and all do.

Unlike the popular run-and-gun game, God has given a plan for life beyond it, if we believe in Jesus and accept Him as Lord and Saviour.

Only He has the power to forgive sin - the cause of death - therefore giving us the opportunity to live eternal lives, without the threat of a deathly storm closing in.

Fortnite relies on human players to enter a game. Each character, regardless of wacky outfit, is controlled by a living being and everyone running (or driving or walking or zip-lining) in every game, faces this same death march. That's sobering to think about the next time you're waiting to drop off the Battle Bus. Don't assume you have more time. Let God do something about your sin problem; confess them to Him and believe in Jesus, now.

Then, no matter how far away the storm of death is, you will have eternal security, which is better than any digital bragging rights or a Victory Umbrella.

> *"For the wages of sin is death, but the free gift of God is eternal life in Christ Jesus our Lord."*
>
> *—Romans 6:23*

See also... Revelation 21:4, Ecclesiastes 12: 7, John 11: 25-26, 1 Corinthians 15:51-57

Title: **Timing is Everything for Frogs and Life**
Game: *Frogger*
Themes: **Guidance, faith**

A JITTERY hand is no good for *Frogger*. It takes relaxed yet precise movements to guide that little blob of green pixels into the five spaces at the top of the screen.

What a simple concept for a game. Get a frog across a busy highway without getting squished. Easy right? Not when the various lanes of traffic move at different speeds and you have to step onto floating logs that disappear beneath the water.

It's never really made clear why falling into the water means death for *Frogger*. After all, aren't frogs able to swim? Then again, why does falling into the water at the bottom of so many games mean certain death?

Maybe video game water is harder than real-world water.

Timing is everything in *Frogger*. Timing can be everything in the real world as well.

It's been said that God tends to work like a set of traffic lights when directing our paths. It can be green for go ahead; get this job done or do that particular project.

It might be orange, suggesting He doesn't want you to commit to something just yet, and maybe not for another few days, months or years even.

Of course, God can say stop as well. We complain about a lack of answer to prayer sometimes but "no" is an answer to.

You won't get far in *Frogger* if you grab the joystick and wildly start pushing the digital amphibian about the place.

Much of the game is about holding back from jumping, waiting for the right opportunity when it appears.

We don't have the bigger picture of the screen that God does. He sees the whole *Frogger* highway, and the raging river beyond that. It makes sense that we listen to Him before leaping ahead.

Exactly how then does God nudge us in the right direction, or hold us back? Through circumstances, through our consciences, through our parents, through verses from the Bible that pop into our heads when confronted with a situation.

You've got to be open to Him, listening for Him and talking to Him. Start to see things as less "just coincidence" and more "God's direction".

There may be a reason you didn't get the top mark for that project (a lesson in humility maybe?) or that your work tools were upgraded sooner than you expected (preparation for a heavier workload to help someone else?).

These things keep us from jumping in front of trucks of recklessness or being snapped by a crocodile of temptation.

Occasionally, we will slip beneath the wheels of that car or drop into the swirling waters by mistake. Believe it or not, there's a reason for that as well.

Valuable lessons can be learned by the way you die in a game like *Frogger*; it sharpens you, makes you alert to that particular danger again. There's a good chance you won't slip-up that way another time.

The old saying "look before you leap" pays dividends in *Frogger*. God wants us to look to Him before we leap.

> *"Trust in the LORD with all your heart, and do not lean on your own understanding. In all your ways acknowledge him, and he will make straight your paths."*
>
> —*Proverbs 3: 5-6*

See also… 2 Thessalonians 3:5; Psalm 119: 105; Psalm 37:23

Title: **Cut for the Better**
Game: *Fruit Ninja*
Themes: **God's word**

FEW of us will ever get the opportunity of slicing through truckloads of fruit hurled from below with a razor sharp sword.

It's certainly a lot less messy (not to mention safer) to do exactly that on *Fruit Ninja*, than in real life.

There is a great sense of power, even stress relief, that comes from swiping one's finger across a soaring watermelon and seeing it split in two.

One of the features to the game which gives it such appeal is the accurate detail shown of what's inside the fruit. The right coloured juice spills out and even the seeds can be seen.

The Bible is a sword. It's given that description in Ephesians 6 as part of the armour of God (see the devotion on *Wonder Boy III: The Dragon's Trap, p108*) but Hebrews 12 gives a more intricate picture of it.

It describes it as "sharper than a two-edged sword". Reading the Bible and taking in what it says, affects a person; it changes them.

This is God's word after all, not just another book. It's God speaking directly to the reader, an open line of communication.

But here's the thing. While we might like to think of this *Fruit Ninja* analogy as using God's word to slice through opposition and "attack" non-believers, consider a different angle.

Imagine that you are the fruit. Okay, so it might be difficult to picture yourself as a soaring strawberry, an aloft apple or a plunging pineapple, but think beyond that and the Bible as a cutting blade, a two-edged sword as it were.

It misses nothing and it cuts deep. It exposes what's inside us, in all its detail, piercing our souls to show what lurks beneath.

And that's not a bad thing. The Bible shows the standard that God expects, and how none of us measure up to it.

Thankfully, it also reveals God's deep and penetrating love for us, even though we are rotten to the core, He still loves us and is willing to forgive our wretched acts and thoughts through Jesus' sacrifice.

Have you let the Bible slice you open? Do you read God's word enough to be cut by it, challenged, changed, sent in a new direction?

Fruit isn't fully enjoyed or fulfilling its purpose until it is sliced open. The same goes for humans.

Throw yourself before God and let him slice and dice you into a new person.

"For the word of God is living and active, sharper than any two-edged sword, piercing to the division of soul and of spirit, of joints and of marrow, and discerning the thoughts and intentions of the heart."

—Hebrews 4:12

See also… Hebrews 4:13; Jeremiah 23:29; Ephesians 6:17; 1 Corinthians 14:25

Title: **The Bombardment of Temptations**
Game: *Galaga*
Themes: **Temptation**

GALAGA is a game that seems like it'll never stop.

It is a constant bombardment of hostile aliens (that curiously look like moths and bees) descending down on you, like so many other space-themed games and rip-offs.

They duck and weave and curl, ever coming for you in a cascade of brightly-coloured menace.

Temptations can be no different.

We think we have the patterns worked out, but then they find a new way to bombard us and shimmy around our defences, no matter how quick we think we are.

That small bit of gossip we know; that unpleasant thought about a person; that program/show we've just downloaded that we didn't pay for- those things that stir your conscience and make you feel uneasy- they're temptations.

It's vital to keep an eye out for the "aliens of temptations" that creep up behind you.

These are the ones that are off screen for a moment, or out of consideration in your life currently, which may just happen to flick back onto your radar without warning.

In *Galaga*, there is a capture beam fired by an enemy ship that, if you're caught by it, seems to rob you of a life.

If you're captured by a temptation, a slave to it, it'll rob you of life as it consumes all you do.

There are temptations that seem controllable, then at the last minute they fire an extra shot.

It could be that "one extra drink" or that "little bit of innocent flirting". Just because you conquer one doesn't mean a hundred others aren't already descending, *Galaga*-style.

As you play along in life, new ones crop up, like aliens you've not seen before, moving and slithering in ways you haven't encountered.

It all sounds so imposing. But then, so does a wall of neatly arranged insect-aliens hovering above you when all you've got is a single-firing spaceship.

Temptations need to be shut down, or shot down in spaceship terms, before they get close. Move out of the way and don't get touched by them.

What ammunition should you use against temptation you may ask? Prayer is a big one, as is Bible memorisation.

Loading up on verses that can be fired when something sinister appears is a definite winner. God promises to help us in times of temptation, and better yet, says we won't be tempted beyond what we can take.

In *Galaga* terms; there'll never be more aliens on the screen than we can handle.

It's only with God's guiding steady hand that you can overcome them and shut them down.

> *"No temptation has overtaken you that is not common to man. God is faithful, and He will not let you be tempted beyond your ability, but with the temptation He will also provide the way of escape, that you may be able to endure it."*
>
> —*1 Corinthians 10:13*

See also… James 1: 12-16; Matthew 6:13

Title: **The Danger of Dabbling**
Game: *Golden Axe*
Themes: **The occult**

THREE hardened warriors, bristling with muscles and brandishing powerful weapons, leap, run, shoulder charge and cut their way through hordes of opposing forces on their way to secure the Golden Axe.

They also kick small elves.

Amid all that power, at the end of a long day of battling evil, they appear to love nothing more than sinking the boot into some otherwise innocent and harmless creatures who cough up bottles of magic potion from their sacks. Collect enough of these and your magic metre grows.

Then, in a tight situation, you can call on other-worldly magic to intervene in various ways including lightning bolts, fire and a volcano, depending on which character you chose.

There are those who take a similar approach in the real world, hoping for real magic solutions to a crisis. There is no denying a spiritual realm exists. The Bible talks about demons in very real terms. It also has plenty to say about avoiding getting involved in matters of the occult.

Many people, supposed clairvoyants, palm readers, aura illustrators and so forth, appear to provide an easy solution or a sense of hope.

Some are clearly charlatans but others may very well be tapping into dark forces which they have no control over.

In *Golden Axe*, the magic happens, the enemies (or troubles in life) are punished and all seems well for a moment but before long it's back to the grind as more opposing forces swarm in.

A false spiritual offering/solution can do the same; all might seem well for a stint until things go bad again. There is a deeper concern that it is dabbling in areas God has warned against.

In Deuteronomy, He gives a strong "heads up" to the children of Israel to avoid worshiping the Gods of the Canaanites or the other tribes. We should look to God as our help first and foremost. He has promised to never leave us nor forsake us (Hebrews 13:5), regardless if the skeletons, trolls, ogres or giants of life keep on attacking us. He has not promised to make life easy or to smooth every path however, unlike some indicators of those peddling crystals or spells or life tricks.

We can call on the Holy Spirit for help but don't expect the head of a dragon to appear from above and rage fire down upon the landscape.

In Psalm 121 we read: "I lift up my eyes to the hills. From where does my help come? My help comes from the Lord, who made heaven and earth."

That's where ours should come from as well, not from an unknown, hollow promise of a soothsayer (an old word used for fortune teller).

For anything that appears to deal with matters of a spiritual nature it's worth asking: How does it align with the Word of God? Anything not in sync with that should be avoided.

Best to double tap in the other direction and run away from it.

"There shall not be found among you anyone who burns his son or his daughter as an offering, anyone who practices divination or tells fortunes or interprets omens, or a sorcerer or a charmer or a medium or a necromancer or one who inquires of the dead."

—Deuteronomy 18:10–11

See also... Psalm 101:3; Leviticus 19:31; Isaiah 8:19; Ephesians 6:10-12

Title: **Tune-Ups Required**
Game: *Gran Turismo*
Themes: **Lifestyle**

A FRIEND was talking about his obsession with *Gran Turismo* when it first came out on the PlayStation.

He and his brothers (all adults) got heavily involved with it, beyond just a casual race every now and again.

He recalls that they would meet up and spend hours racing each other before going back to their individual homes and continue racing in order to find new ways to improve their cars.

Hours, he says, were spent refining parts to their cars; changing tyres, adjusting braking systems, altering transmissions and so forth, all to give them a slight edge when they met up again to play.

Back in those days (which makes it seem like a hundred years ago) they would save their cars onto a memory card and carry them around, just in case they went somewhere that had a PlayStation and a challenger.

Gran Turismo boasts it is the "real driving simulator".

Even though it's a video game that's accessible to everyone, you could almost step back and say: "It's not a toy."

The cars are based on actual cars, set in the real world. To be successful, a player can't just jump into the driver's seat, press the accelerator to the floor and easily navigate all the corners.

There are physics and elements at play which make it feel real and require practise and adjustments to really appreciate the finesse of the game.

Yes, you can "jump right into the car" of the Christian life (salvation is instantaneous) but that doesn't mean you'll be automatically able to negotiate every tricky corner or challenge that comes along.

An old Sunday School song has the line: "Little by little everyday, little by little in every way, Jesus is changing me."

Growth isn't a fast process. Yes, there is a major change in a person's life when they accept Jesus as their Lord and Saviour but becoming more like Him takes time.

It can be about making those adjustments and refinements; shaking off the clothes of the old life and embracing the new-found God-given freedom from sin.

In some circumstances, an entirely new car is called for. A complete change in thinking could be needed in your life once you give it to God.

The old things that used to hold such an attraction just aren't designed for the new track in life you are now on.

Actually, it will be God Himself, the great mechanic, who will do the refining and adjusting in your life. Better yet, let Him take the wheel completely. (No memory card required.)

> *"But that is not the way you learned Christ! - assuming that you have heard about him and were taught in him, as the truth is in Jesus, to put off your old self, which belongs to your former manner of life and is corrupt through deceitful desires, and to be renewed in the spirit of your minds, and to put on the new self, created after the likeness of God in true righteousness and holiness."*
>
> *—Ephesians 4: 20-24*

See also… 2 Corinthians 5:17; Colossians 3: 8-11; Romans 12: 2; Ephesians 2:10

Title: **The Rhythm of Praise**
Game: *Guitar Hero*
Themes: **Praise**

Psalm 150: 3-5 says: *"Praise Him with the sounding of the trumpet, praise Him with the harp and lyre, praise Him with timbrel and dancing, praise Him with the strings and pipe, praise Him with the clash of cymbals, praise Him with resounding cymbals."*

IT'S like the writer is encouraging the reader to form a band and get busy praising God.

Almost.

Not everyone has the money, talent and garage space to launch a band.

Enter: *Guitar Hero*.

PlayStation II owners suddenly became honed guitar slingers adored by millions of (digitally rendered) screaming fans, all within their lounge-rooms or bedrooms.

A rhythm-based game, various coloured "notes" stream toward the player who has to press the corresponding coloured button on the plastic guitar-shaped controller, and sometimes do strumming via the strum bar or add an extra embellishment with the "whammy bar" (no really, that's what it's called).

The guitar was one of the first before various other accessories came out to complete the band feel, including drum kits and keyboards.

Had there been a Psalm 150 version of *Guitar Hero*, there could quite possibly have been a plastic lyre, timbrel, harp and trumpet accessories to go along with it.

Guitar Hero taps into that inner urge many people have to be a rockstar.

Humans have a natural affinity with music, it seems. God wired it into us, perhaps for the very praise of Him.

There are no high scores for praising Jesus; no standards that must be achieved in order that He will get the glory. In other words; you don't have to sing in tune to tell Him you love Him.

Of course, singing, listening to or playing music aren't the only ways to praise Him but they sure are an enjoyable, natural way.

Songs and music that glorify God help keep our thoughts on Him rather than have them stray into the things of the world.

As fun as they are, there's no need to have the wireless Les Paul Gibson replica guitar to give God the glory, nor even the pitch perfect voice of a lead singer.

God wants to hear from your heart first and foremost. So it's not so much about making music to rock on; it's about giving thanks for the rock you are on.

"Let everything that has breath praise the Lord. Praise the Lord!"

—Psalm 150:6

See also… Deuteronomy 3:24; Psalm 98; Isaiah 38:20; 1 Chronicles 13:8, 15-16

Title: Regurgitating Evil Into Good
Game: Kirby's Adventure
Themes: Evil to good

THERE is a strange juxtaposition in *Kirby's Adventure*; even stranger than using the word, juxtaposition, within the first line of a video games devotional.

On one hand, the game is drippingly sweet in its innocence.

Kirby appears to be a pink, merry, cuddly marshmallow going through levels with equally placid names like Vegetable Island and Ice Cream Island. The jingly music bops along as if all is right in the world.

All this softness though is balanced against the action and controls.

The bad guys come at Kirby with all sorts of attacks.

Swords, fireballs and electricity are just some of the not-so-nice weapons with which the nasties of Dream Land try to hurt the title character.

Kirby meets it all head-on though, not shirking his/her (it's hard to know exactly what Kirby's gender is, so we'll go for female) responsibility to find the parts of the Dream Rod, enabling the inhabitants of Dream Land to dream once more.

Kirby has a vast array of skills to call upon, many of which she "steals" from her enemies.

The concept of being able to take an enemy's attack and use it to progress reminds us of the story of Joseph (the one with the colourful coat).

Years after his brothers had sold him out of jealousy, Joseph wound up in Egypt and rose through the ranks to have the top job next to the pharaoh.

Eventually, drought forces his brothers to come groveling to him after their father, Jacob, had died. He accepts them warmly though and delivers this line in verse 20: "You intended to harm me, but God intended it for good to accomplish what is now being done, the saving of many lives."

God took something that was intended for wrong and used it for His holy purposes, like the enemy attack methods against Kirby, who uses them for the bigger purpose of her mission.

God has continually done this all throughout history, weaving a larger tapestry out of the seemingly evil things man concocts to make good come about.

The ultimate example of this of course is the crucifixion and resurrection of Jesus, where many thought killing the one who claimed to be the Son of God would end His earthly work.

Rather, it was always part of God's plan and His very death provided the means for the forgiveness of sin, so we might have a relationship with Him again; it's the very definition of Good News.

Don't despair at the evil in the world or even at the seemingly bad times you're experiencing.

God can orchestrate something positive from it through His grace and love.

Although it may be a bit hard to swallow (terrible Kirby pun there), know that God has defeated His enemies already and whatever they serve up will become tools to progress His plan further.

> *"As for you, you meant evil against me, but God meant it for good, to bring it about that many people should be kept alive, as they are today."*
>
> *—Genesis 50:20*

See also… Romans 8:28; Ephesians 5:13, 1 Corinthians 15:28; Philippians 2:13

Title: Marching Toward Death
Game: *Lemmings*
Themes: Death

LEMMINGS (the digital video game versions at least) seem drawn to death.

Maybe it's not an attraction to death but the simple fact they don't know what lies ahead.

The creatures within *Lemmings* have no regard at all for their own safety, bobbing along to the beat of some catchy tunes (including *"How Much is That Doggy in the Window?"*), happy to follow the one in front, even if that means falling off a cliff or being minced up in a kind of violent turnstile.

The countdown timer gives a sense of urgency to the player's rescue mission, as he or she races to save the required percentage of lemmings. There isn't much time to rescue as many as possible.

Action is the key. It's no good simply watching their impending doom, feeling sad and wishing they'd turn aside from what's to come.

Now, swap in lemmings for your friends and family in the real world.

Okay, so not many of the humans you know have green hair and wear purple jumpsuits but it is true that every human you know is headed toward death.

Many humans have no regard for their own spiritual safety, ambling along not knowing what lies ahead. They simply "do not know what they do" (Luke 23:34).

Ecclesiastes 7 says that death is the destiny for everyone. Why is that? Why are we all sentenced to die, like lemmings into a pit of lava?

The book of Romans says the "wages of sin is death". The same book also says that all have sinned, and when you think about it, that's true. Every single person has done something wrong at some point in their lives, which means they are a sinner, which means they are separated from the perfect God.

It's not exactly a pleasant dinner conversation so perhaps that's why so many don't know.

But because God loves His creation, humans, so much, He came up with a plan to save them. That plan included Jesus dying on the cross to pay the price for all of our sins, so that we might mend that relationship with God and even have eternal life

It's like finding that gateway in every level that all the creatures happily tumble into.

Those who know this and are saved have been given a job to do; to let people know about the danger ahead and the need to turn from sin.

That might mean using different strategies in the lives of those around you to make an impact, to try to stop them from doing something, to find them a new direction, to build a bridge over a danger.

In the game, the eight "tasks" you can assign to the lemmings are action tasks; things that will influence their direction and destiny.

God does the saving; He created the final destination and the way out but how can you be a builder, a digger, a stopper to direct people to Jesus for salvation? Let's go!

> "The sting of death is sin, and the power of sin is the law. But thanks be to God, who gives us the victory through our Lord Jesus Christ."
>
> —*1 Corinthians 15: 56-57*

See also… Romans 13: 11; 1 Peter 4: 7; John 11: 15-26

Title: **Small Acts, Big Impacts**
Game: *Little Big Planet*
Themes: **Serving, works**

SOFT, spongy, no opposable digits, an overly large head and a cumbersome zipper down his front.

Add the name, Sackboy and he really doesn't sound like a hero to save the day.

No gun on his side, no bazooka on his shoulder, not even a cape; just him and his abilities to jump and grab onto things. It's not exactly the extreme skillset that is going to set the gaming world alight.

Despite all this, *Little Big Planet* is a big game. Its soft furnishings and easy gameplay make it appealing for so many boys, girls, teens, grown-ups, hardcore gamers and casual dippers.

Heroes come in funny forms. Think about the more offbeat heroes in books, film and the Bible:

- *Frodo:* A short, hairy-footed Hobbit takes a ring a long way to destroy it.
- *Napoleon Dynamite*: An ultra nerd and social outcast who stands up for his friend and helps him win an election.
- *Atticus Finch*: The humble American lawyer in *To Kill a Mockingbird* that represents the under-represented in the courtroom.
- *Daredevil*: The Marvel comic hero who is blind lawyer, Matthew Murdoch, with heightened senses and combats injustice in a red suit.

- *Moses*: A bloke who says he isn't very good at public speaking but eventually leads the children of Israel out of Egypt from under the Pharaoh's nose.
- *Saul/Paul*: From going out of his way to kill Christians, to becoming a Christian revolutionary himself.
- *Jesus*: A carpenter, born in an animal shelter, who cares for people and eventually dies for humanity, rises again, and in doing so, conquers sin.

These are some of the stories that give people hope. Perhaps people can relate to Sackboy?

Very few of us are built like comic superheroes or have grand powers.

Jesus was God in human form but was also fully man, so we can relate to Him.

We aren't necessarily called to be heroes in others' lives but sometimes the small things have big impacts.

The Bible records plenty of miracles Jesus did on earth like turning water into wine, raising people from the dead, walking on water and calming a storm, but it also notes plenty of day-to-day stuff alongside it.

He interacted with people, told stories, listened to them and shared meals. In fact there are probably more accounts of Jesus doing daily life, almost boring stuff, than there are big ticket eye-opening events.

We're not called to be miracle workers but to be salt and light; down-to-earth, everyday sort of people showing God's love for others through practical (physically helping out or interacting) and spiritual (praying for) means.

Perhaps Sackboy's tasks don't seem that big (ie. Saving lamps for genies, getting pizza for dragons) but they are important to those for whom he is impacting.

He's not necessarily trying to change the world; he's just tackling each individual situation as it presents itself.

When it comes to serving God practically, there's no need to be a Mega Man; there's hope in just being a Sackboy (or girl, of course.)

> *"For truly, I say to you, whoever gives you a cup of water to drink because you belong to Christ will by no means lose his reward."*
>
> —*Mark 9:41*

See also… Matthew 5: 16; James 2: 15-17; Luke 3: 11; 1 John 3: 18

Title: **Forgive and Accelerate**
Game: ***Mario Kart***
Themes: **Growth, forgiveness**

THAT thunderbolt is a right so-and-so.

Striking from nowhere, it rains down pain upon the unsuspecting racer, causing his/her/its vehicle to spin out of control for a few moments, losing precious racing time.

They come at the worst possible time too, just as you're defying gravity or while jumping a sand island.

The thunderbolt can be the difference between winning and losing in *Mario Kart*.

It is the epitome of something being beyond one's control. Even worse than that, it is caused by someone else, another player, someone you might not even see.

People - those we don't know, have never met or are unlikely to ever meet - may do things or make decisions which impact on our own lives for what seems the worst.

These situations strike us perhaps when we least expect it. That can be financial (losing a job); emotional (posting something unkind directly related to you); mental (that complex calculus question you just can't master); or even political (the introduction of a new law which doesn't make sense to you).

It seems the good *Mario Kart* players are the ones who, when they get hit, are already preparing to forge on, to plant the accelerator, to make it to that final flag.

The apostle Paul speaks about striving towards a goal, pressing on towards the finish, which is to be more like Jesus.

He says although we are afflicted, we are not crushed; perplexed but not driven to despair; struck down but not destroyed.

In other words, we might take a hit from a thunderbolt or a tortoise shell (ie. Someone might make fun of us for being a Christian or accuse us of being religious) but it's important we keep the accelerator button flat and keep going forward.

Living a Christian life means there is plenty of opposition out there.

If Jesus was playing *Mario Kart*, He wouldn't waste time pursuing the person who shot at Him or left the banana peel on the road dead ahead; He'd forgive and accelerate.

You will waste valuable time holding a grudge or waiting for payback - better to forgive and accelerate.

> *"Put on then, as God's chosen ones, holy and beloved, compassionate hearts, kindness, humility, meekness, and patience, bearing with one another and, if one has a complaint against another, forgiving each other; as the Lord has forgiven you, so you also must forgive."*
>
> —*Colossians 3: 12 - 13*

See also… 2 Corinthians 4:8-12; Mark 11: 25-26

Title: **The Power of Peace**
Game: *Metal Gear Solid*
Themes: **Peace**

THERE is a great story of stealth in the Bible. 1 Samuel tells of King Saul trying to hunt down David who is on the run in the wilderness.

King Saul gets together about 3000 soldiers and heads off to find David and probably do something unpleasant to him.

On the way there, Saul has to "attend to his needs" (ie. go to the bathroom/toilet) which he does so in a cave.

It just so happens David and his crew are camped in some caves nearby. David sees Saul in the cave, sneaks up on him but instead of killing him, he cuts off a piece of his robe.

Later Saul finds out about this and is overwhelmed by the fact David could have killed him, but didn't.

You can imagine David crawling like Solid Snake in *Metal Gear Solid*.

The game helped elevate what's known as the stealth genre; it's all about patience and remaining unseen.

God doesn't ask us to remain unseen. In fact, He tells us the opposite, but there is a lesson to be learned from how Solid Snake interacts.

It is possible to complete some of the challenges within the *Metal Gear Solid* games without killing an enemy.

Think about that; so many video games are about shooting a gun, swinging a sword or navigating an army to destroy someone else.

Yet here is one that allows you to get through by avoiding conflict.

Solid Snake has all the gear; guns, tools, a special suit, radio support; but he is good at what he does because he shows power in restraint.

By not blasting away with a gun or tearing someone apart with a knife when he has the opportunity, he shows control over the power he has, just like David did. He could have knocked Saul's head off but he didn't.

Jesus was the same, showing power in restraint. On many occasions when people got up in His face He could have simply deleted them from existence. He is God, afterall.

Instead, He engaged them in peace. The Bible says the Son of God came into the world to save it, not condemn it.

Do you engage people in peace? Show power through restraint? Despite what society may think, we don't always have to have the upper hand over people or have the most power in the room.

Even though we might have an arsenal of comeback lines, terrifying glares or even two fists that could really do some rearranging, they will do more damage to our Christian witness than we can serve up to the person who is annoying us.

Try infiltrating someone's guard by showing love.

"Turn away from evil and do good; seek peace and pursue it."

—*Psalm 34:14*

See also… Galatians 5: 22-23; John 14: 27; Romans 12:18; Hebrews 12:14

Title: **Special Beneath the Suit**
Game: *Metroid*
Themes: **Women**

SPOILER ALERT: For anyone who has not played, and completed the original *Metroid*, this article reveals the ending. Of course, it's pretty well known among gaming circles by now but just in case, it was thought best to give fair warning.

It is regarded as one of the biggest twists or shocks in video game history. *Metroid*, released on the Nintendo Entertainment System in 1986, sees an almost robot-like character sent to a planet to rid it of a nasty alien species.

New skills and weapons are picked up along the way.

Then at the end, if completed in a certain time, the main character, Samus, removes the helmet to reveal… she is a woman.

It was a bold move at the time when female lead characters were few and far between. (Some would argue not much has changed.)

Samus does heroic things throughout the game; running and leaping and solving puzzles and turning into a ball thing.

She travels to a planet in order to save it (a very Jesus-like thing to do).

She adapts and uses what she has been given, which is exactly the way God designed women in the first place.

There are plenty of heroic females within the Bible; Deborah, Mary, Martha, Miriam, Esther, Ruth, Naaman's servant girl and Jael, who drove a tent peg through the head of Sisera, commander of the Canaanite army, while he was asleep. (Is this where the term, "a splitting headache", comes from?)

God made women to have a special role, not a lesser role within the world. Women and men are meant to work together, to complement each other in bringing glory to God.

God's not into stereotyping. If anything, He's usually breaking that mould, like using the weak to achieve big things or sinful people to bring about His purposes.

We can often view women as the weaker gender. It is true God made them not as physically strong as men but they are far from being less capable, important or significant.

In Matthew 23, Jesus even uses the idea of one of the most lowly of female creatures, a hen, to illustrate God's yearning to save His people by suggesting He has "longed to gather your children together, as a hen gathers her chicks under her wings".

In a world that increasingly celebrates machoism and seems to give power to men, the Bible continually reminds us of the strength of women.

They don't all wear a power suit but they still do remarkable things, just as God intended them to.

> *"Nevertheless, in the Lord woman is not independent of man nor man of woman; for as woman was made from man, so man is now born of woman. And all things are from God."*
>
> —*1 Corinthians 11:11-12*

See also… Proverbs 31:30, Galatians 3:28, Proverbs 31:16-17, Proverbs 31:20-21

Title: **Credit to the Creator**
Game: ***Minecraft***
Themes: **Creation**

THERE is a certain freedom to *Minecraft*. Players are really only limited by their imaginations as to what they can design, make and use.

But you can't invent a new block for yourself.

You have to use that which is within the game. God has given us the building blocks of life. It may be hard for some scientists to swallow but everything we create and re-design is originally from God in the first place.

There is an old joke where a group of scientists are having a conversation with God, claiming they can build a human being as well as He can.

He challenges them to a human-making competition. The group of scientists gather up a handful of dirt to begin, to which God replies: "Get your own dirt."

The *Minecraft* community conjures up all sorts of worlds and challenges. There are games within games as people put together mazes, traps and rollercoasters. Some have re-created entire real-world cities (ie. Denmark) on a scale-for-scale model.

But none of this would be possible without the original rules of the game itself. You can't say you're playing *Minecraft* but just stare at a blank screen.

By investing time in it, by being a player, you are acknowledging the game's creator, even if the object of the game is about creating more stuff. Confused? Don't be.

The point is God deserves acknowledgement as the creator of life. As humans, we may think we are clever with what we come up with and how we heal ourselves but at the base of it, we are only using what God has given us. It seems crazy to think that *Minecraft* just developed all by itself, or even that the initial landscape just happened to be there.

If you've had anything to do with computers or consoles or games, you'll know that very little is based on random calculations. Even those things that do appear random are driven by a computer calculating randomness.

There is a design underlying all of it; how things fit together, the rules of play, the need to do some things first before other things can happen.

As a designer, God's intricate plans are far beyond what we can comprehend, that's why some people end up going along with the notion of life evolving from one stage to another without an intelligent basis.

It's worth remembering our Creator God when encountering something incredible in life.

It doesn't have to be that tranquil rainforest or the cliche of seeing an eagle in the wild. It could be the miracle of modern technology, the fact you are holding a wireless controller in your hand or how electricity is manipulated to create another world on screen.

God has made it all possible. Take the time to thank Him for it.

> *"The heavens declare the glory of God, and the sky above proclaims his handiwork."*
>
> —*Psalm 19: 1*

See also… Isaiah 40: 22-23; Romans 1: 20

Title: **Treading Too Carefully**
Game: ***Minesweeper***
Themes: **Sharing the Gospel**

VERY few people play just a single game of *Minesweeper*. One turn is usually followed immediately by another because "I've got the hang of it now".

Minesweeper used to come as a free game on personal computers and provided a quick flash of amusement to those meant to be working or doing homework.

Players are presented with a grid which they have to click on in order to reveal numbers that indicate how many "mines" are surrounding that number.

Squares which contain suspected mines can be "red flagged". The idea is to reveal all the squares leaving only the red-flagged squares with mines in them.

Clicking on a mine means game over, as it triggers all the mines to erupt/reveal.

There is an instant nervousness which comes with this game. Does that square contain a mine? Should it be clicked on? What are the numbers indicating?

That same nervousness often grips us when it comes to sharing the Gospel with someone.

What will they say? What if now's not the right time? What if they explode at being "clicked on"?

As we get to know a person, they reveal what they are like, their beliefs and tendencies, and we can end up red-flagging certain areas we believe are "no go" zones because it might trigger something.

Minesweeper has a time limit. You can stare at the grid all day, doubting, questioning, second-guessing, wondering what the exact right square is to click, and then the time runs out and all is lost anyway.

It is possible to tread too carefully.

It takes a bold approach to go forth and reveal the Good News of God's love to a person.

We simply don't know how long anyone has in this world. That should drive us to be confident in telling people about Christ despite the possibility of an explosion.

The Bible is full of examples of those who shared God's message and had people blow up in their faces for hearing it (ie. John the Baptist, Phillip, Noah, Daniel).

Fear can hold us back from sharing but if every life has a time limit on it anyway, the need to talk to them about the way of salvation should override that fear. In fact, the fear could simply be our own selfishness because we are afraid the person will no longer like us for our faith.

Being bold in sharing your faith doesn't mean being reckless of course. Paul urged his followers to be "wise in the way you act toward outsiders" (Colossians 4:5).

Don't hold back from talking to others about God for fear of a hidden mine.

The clock is ticking.

"Continue steadfastly in prayer, being watchful in it with thanksgiving. At the same time, pray also for us, that God may open to us a door for the word, to declare the mystery of Christ, on account of which I am in prison - that I may make it clear, which is how I ought to speak. Walk in wisdom toward outsiders, making the best use of the time."

—Colossians 4: 2-5

See also… 2 Timothy 1:8-9; Romans 10: 14-15; Acts 14: 3-4

Title: **Atmospheric Emotions**
Game: *Myst*
Themes: **Emotions**

THERE is no denying it - it's a slow game.

In this day and age of ultra-smooth graphics and hyper-action titles, *Myst*, the first-person click-and-solve puzzler, seems a world away.

There is no violence here, no heart-pounding boss encounters or race against the clock. It's largely about walking around an island finding solutions to tasks and piecing together a backstory.

At the heart of it is a family mystery that you are burdened with solving, not just for curiosity's sake but also as a means of getting back to your own world.

So there's a lot riding on your Nancy Drew abilities.

It was released in 1993 and since then, computer game makers have become experts at creating in-game atmospheres and emotional connections with players.

Myst though, seemed to be one of the first to do an excellent job at establishing an immersive environment that made the player want to keep pressing on to get to the finish.

Myst doesn't push your reflexes or hone your button-pressing prowess; it stretches your brain.

The depth of the puzzles that need solving means a player won't be skipping through it in a casual 20 minutes.

For its time, the images are rich and detailed. But the thing that *Myst* does is make a player *feel* something. It surrounds the participant with ambience, enveloping him or her into the world where the ocean is heard sloshing against the shore, where buttons and levers make unusual clunks or snapping sounds.

You can almost feel the breeze in that spindly pine forest and smell the mustiness of the library as you chase down pages.

On another level within that, the storyline and acting pull the player in different directions of allegiance. Which brother do you believe? Who is lying? How will a wrong decision affect the outcome?

It is easy to become distracted by simply "being in" the game to the point of forgetting about the job at hand.

Feelings have a tendency to do that. God gives us feelings and emotions in the first place but like many good things in this world, they can be manipulated for wrong purposes in a fallen world.

Advertising and marketing teams have gotten emotional connection down to an art. They want customers to fall in love with their brand/product/service.

Even at a more personal level, many people are good manipulators of emotions, knowing what to say in order to get a reaction, or to try and win over someone, often with half-truths and vagaries.

Doing so may not always be beneficial for those trying to live for God.

The Bible says to walk in the Spirit in order to avoid succumbing to false emotional appeals.

Be alert to when the emotional atmosphere of a situation could be leading you down a harmful path, even if it's a beautifully rendered digital island.

"But I say, walk by the Spirit, and you will not gratify the desires of the flesh."

—Galatians 5: 16

See also… 1 John 2: 16; Proverbs 3: 5 - 6; 1 Corinthians 10: 13

Title: Trying to Outrun Sin
Game: PAC-Man
Themes: Sin, forgiveness

NOTHING induces panic quite like those coloured ghosts getting faster and coming after you.

At the start of every level of *PAC-Man*, there are a daunting number of dots to chew up, and not nearly enough Power Pellets to turn you into a ghost-chomping champion.

Of course, adding to these challenges are those pink, blue, red and orange ghosts (actually named Pinky, Inky, Blinky, and Clyde) who just keep on hunting you down.

At no point in the original game do PAC-Man and the ghosts sit down for a cup of coffee and negotiate what's fair.

Sin tends to lurk in our lives like that; it keeps coming back. No matter how old we are or what we do, we can't seem to outrun it, and it relentlessly tries to catch up with us.

There are times when we might think we are getting ahead of it, even turning to a Power Pellet (work, holidays, a hobby, a relationship, etc) to try to gobble it up but sooner or later, that wears off, and its true colours re-emerge.

What's worse, it comes back to bite us.

Humans are born with a sin nature so it would be unfair to just say "make good decisions in life, take the right turns and just avoid sin".

"Just avoid the ghosts" isn't exactly sparkling advice for a *PAC-Man* player.

God can't ignore sin. He knows those ghosts exist in our lives. He sees them even more clearly than we do.

God has dealt with them though. Call it the ultimate Power Pellet if you like, but through Jesus' death and resurrection, He's conquered sin.

It need not be the creeping, edging, lurking sense of uneasiness that it is or was.

He also knows we are human and can't outrun it. So He forgives… and forgives and forgives and forgives.

You don't go into *PAC-Man* wanting to die. You don't plunge into the game and head straight for the ghosts to see if they really will come back; we know they will.

Once you've accepted Jesus as your Lord and Saviour, you don't go chasing sin to test God's forgiveness.

We know sin is going to keep coming for us, so we do our best to stay out of its way.

But it's nice to know that should we make a slip, take a wrong turn or even sit in the same place for too long and a ghost of sin finds us, we can take it to God where forgiveness will be granted and removed, as far as the east is from the west.

> *"As far as the east is from the west, so far does He remove our transgressions from us,"*
>
> *—Psalm 103: 12*

See also… Psalm 103: 10; Matthew 6: 12; 1 John 1: 8-10

Title: Worth Clinging To
Game: *Pitfall!*
Themes: Scripture

IN 1982, video games didn't exactly boast orchestral scores (music). The hardware didn't have the capacity to replicate such scores anyway but designers did the best they could.

Pitfall! (Yes, it's spelt with an exclamation mark at the end of it) doesn't have a rolling tune behind it. Rather it has selected special effects when various things happen such as collecting a treasure or treading on a log.

Those who play it (or have played it) will know one of the recurring bits of audio is that electronic midi sound which sort-of replicates Tarzan's call when Pitfall Harry swings on a vine.

A player will hear it a lot because swinging on vines is nearly a must to get through this side-scroller in order to collect all 32 treasures within the allocated 20 minutes. (Curiously, nothing happens once all are collected. The game goes to a "kill screen" whereby it freezes, and that's it, leaving the player to ask so many questions, including what happens to all that collected treasure?)

Think of the vines as memorised Bible verses. Yes, they can be thought of as just being "handy" but they are also essential. Knowing scripture will help you through difficult times.

They aren't magic spells though. It's not about chanting them or reciting them and waiting for a puff of smoke and an instant solution.

Some verses are practical in nature, like James 4:7 which says to "surrender to God, resist the devil, and he will run from you", and many of the Proverbs have sensible advice about wisdom and relationships. Others will be more educational and informative, telling about God's deep love which should provide reassurance and hope. Others still will be inspirational, such as the Psalms or Song of Solomon (or even Ecclesiastes or Lamentations when fully digested).

Not many people will be able to have a mental catalogue of verses to call upon in each situation but any memorised part of scripture will be better than nothing.

There is reassurance and peace to be had simply knowing the words are directly from God Himself, to you.

Pitfall Harry faces some unexpected obstacles. Pits, both blue and black, sometimes just open up then fade away, making it tricky to negotiate.

A vine will provide a clear path across but Harry has to use it. He could try to go it alone but more often than not that will result in getting chomped on by a crocodile, burnt by a fire, stung by a scorpion or vanishing down one of those sinkholes.

While Harry strives to collect the bars of sparkling gold or silver, rings and bags of money, perhaps the real treasures are the vines, the things that truly preserve his life and get him through.

If we treasure our Bible verses, they will become like valued items to us as well, ready to be called up and clung to.

It will be those verses that resonate within our heads, not an 8-bit audio sting.

"Let the word of Christ dwell in you richly, teaching and admonishing one another in all wisdom, singing psalms and hymns and spiritual songs, with thankfulness in your hearts to God."

—Colossians 3:16

See also… 2 Timothy 3: 16-17; Psalm 119:11; Deuteronomy 11:18; Joshua 1:8

Title: **Don't Make Light of Light**
Game: **Plants vs Zombies**
Themes: **God's purity**

"THE zombies… are coming."

Or so murmurs a husky, near-death voice which sends a nervous jitter down your legs as you wonder to yourself; have I done enough to prepare for what's on its way?

And then they come, meandering toward your precious home, jostling their way forward as your carefully (and some not so carefully) selected plants spit out peas or cabbages or punch the onslaught that's coming.

And while all this is going on, you're frantically gathering sunshine; those happy round parcels of relief that pop out of sunflowers or descend from above.

They are what's keeping you going. Just a few more and you can plant something better, reinforce your defence.

You need light, both in the game and in life.

The world wouldn't be much fun without the sun. For one, all those solar-powered garden lights would be a waste of time.

The Bible uses light as a reference to truth; something that is revealing, that is clear and pure and holy. No surprises then that it puts it pretty simply: God is light.

Humans seem to have an inbuilt need for light. If we were meant to live in darkness more, wouldn't we have eyes like a cat, or all be given a pair of night-vision goggles when our parents take us home from hospital? That in itself is almost a living metaphor for our spiritual lives: We need God.

We need to know what is truth and embrace that - live by it.

Living in the light is about trying to live as close to God as possible (ie. Prayer, reading the Bible, serving others in love, etc).

The sunshine that falls from some unseen sky in *Plants vs Zombies*, or springs out of sunflowers, just appears. But it's up to us to click on each icon and gather it in.

God makes Himself available but we have to receive Him; click on it, as it were.

Some will be thinking: yes, but what about those levels at night time?

There will be dark times in life; periods where it seems we are alone or abandoned, or where the light doesn't seem as abundant.

That's when light is even more precious and we have to "click on it" even more vigilantly.

The creators of the game provide a way though, just as God does. It might be just the right amount of light you need, the right amount of encouragement, a single word from a friend or a verse you've read or even a song you sang at church to get you through that part.

God's not limited in how He makes Himself known. Live for the light and live in the light.

It will help you face whatever is approaching you, even a zombie bobsled team.

> *"This is the message we have heard from Him and proclaim to you, that God is light, and in Him is no darkness at all."*
>
> *—1 John 1: 5*

See also… 1 John 1: 6-7; 2 Corinthians 4: 6; 1 Peter 2: 9

Title: **Don't Forget to Remember**
Game: *Pokemon*
Themes: **Scripture memorisation**

THERE seemed to be nothing bigger in the world than *Pokemon* in the early 2000s.

Few things captured the attention of children on three levels; toys (figurines, trading cards, costumes), video games (on the highly portable Game Boy) and traditional media (a television cartoon series and animated movies).

Each seemed to fuel the other. Watching the TV series helped you better understand what you were trying to do in the game (both of which could be done while keeping a deck of *Pokemon* cards in your pocket).

It even infiltrated fashion with the main character, Ash Ketchum helping to bring back the popularity of sponge-front trucker caps after they seemed to fall out of vogue.

The game now has many different incarnations and versions but at the heart of *Pokemon* is essentially a collecting game.

It tends to lose some of its appeal when you think about it like that.

If it had been called "Monster Collecting Simulator", it might never have taken off.

Still, players strive to gather and capture as many of the mythical creatures as they can. After all, the catchphrase is: "Gotta catch 'em all!". One practice many Christians find valuable is collecting Bible verses, or as older folk may say, passages of Scripture.

That makes it sound like carrying around small scraps of paper torn from a Bible, but not so.

A collection of key verses can be a tremendous encouragement when things get tough. It's great to be able to call on a bit of the Bible when you need it.

Pokemon players have the trusty Pokedex they can tap into to recall what their most recent captured pocket monster is and what it does.

We probably can't carry around a Pokedex for Bible verses… or can we?

Your brain is better than any imaginary bug indexing system.

Then again, who's to say you can't have a "notes" file on your cell/mobile phone with some key verses jotted down that you can go to when you need reminding of something?

Or perhaps photos of Bible verses you can refer to, or a Bible app for that matter.

Pokemon players enter battles knowing what monsters they have with them.

A memory full of Bible verses can act the same way, helping equip and arm us when we're about to enter into a battle against temptation, against possible lies, against the world's traditional way of doing things.

When it comes to memory verses, it might be a bit ambitious to declare "gotta catch'em all" but still, we might boldly say when a challenge looms: "Scripture, I choose you!"

"I have stored up your word in my heart, that I might not sin against you,"

—Psalm 119: 11

See also… 2 Timothy 3:16; Proverbs 6: 21-22

Title: **Connecting with the Collectors**
Game: *Pokemon Go*
Themes: **Witnessing**

IN parks and malls and other public places around the world, there are individuals and groups of people wandering around like zombies.

Their eyes are fixed on one thing; the small screen in front of them, as they seek those creatures that only exist in pixels on their mobile devices, known as Pokemon.

Pokemon Go had a sudden and incredible impact on the world. Millions signed up for it within days of it being launched.

Its popularity may have waned a little but it is still huge globally.

While it's copped some criticism, it has gotten plenty of people out of their lounges/couches and moving again as they walk to hatch eggs and cover territory to add to their collections.

People are searching for things, and not just Mew or a high level Articuno.

Whether you are into *Pokemon Go* or not, do you ever think that each player standing there, swiping his or her screen and punching the air when he or she wins a gym battle, is one of God's children?

Sadly, they may not know that truth.

There is a longing within people to know there is more to life, to find something that really matters, above money and earthly relationships.

Sometimes it's been referred to as "the God-shaped hole"; that inner need to connect with the Creator.

Pokemon Go provides an opportunity to connect with total strangers in conversation, and in doing so, a chance to share the Good News with them.

Sure, talk Pokemon and gyms and healing potions and incubators, but think about a way to make mention of God, of the One who makes all this technology and the world in which we play it, possible.

In fact, it would be a prime opportunity to bring up the topic of the theory of evolution, to see what their thoughts are and if they've ever considered the reality of an intelligent designer.

We can be seekers of Pokemon ourselves but God has given us a bigger job and that's to be seekers of the lost.

Be prepared though; that's going to take more than raspberries and an Ultra Ball. It's going to take courage, prayer and a reliance on the Holy Spirit to know what to say but it'll be more of an adventure and more rewarding than just adding to an invisible monster collection.

Now is the right time to *Pokemon Go* into all the world.

> *"Then he said to his disciples, 'The harvest is plentiful, but the labourers are few; therefore pray earnestly to the Lord of the harvest to send out labourers into his harvest.'"*
>
> *—Matthew 9:37-38*

See also… Matthew 4:19; 1 Peter 3:15

Title: **The Back and Forth of Evangelism**
Game: *Pong*
Themes: **Evangelism**

DESPITE the name, it's not a game about a wretched stench. *Pong* appears to be derived from ping-pong or table tennis.

The controls are simple; guide a white rectangle up and down on either the far left or right side of the screen to deflect a "ball" (or small white square) as it bounces back and forth, back and forth, back and forth, forth and back, and back and forth.

Ever feel having a disagreement with someone is like a game of *Pong*?

Back and forth, to and fro, serve and receive, point and counterpoint, round and around and around.

The Bible tells us to proclaim the Gospel (Mark 16:15) in the world. In other words, tell everyone we know, and those we don't really know.

Some people, though, simply don't want to hear it. They seem to have a defence against any point given, or a rebuttal to any Bible verse shared.

That small white square just seems to keep coming back, thrown in your face with increasing speed, often with a "point" scored against if you don't have the immediate answer or exact Bible reference. Apologetics is the fancy word for defending the Bible and the Christian faith.

Not everyone has the gift of gently arguing the point but everyone has the ability to share.

Jesus' parable of the sower and the seed (Matthew 13) sees the farmer throw out seed with only one in four of the soils actually taking root.

It's not an exact ratio but if we are throwing out the seed of the Gospel, it seems we can expect the majority of people to not want to hear it, or throw it back in our faces.

Don't despair; playing *Pong* isn't necessarily about ultimate triumph and winning a perfect game, especially when another human player controls the other paddle.

It's about the connection made over the game, the shared moment of interaction.

Perhaps getting a "victory" in an argument isn't the point.

Like a two-player video game, the act of taking the time to engage with that person, even though they may not agree, says they are worth your time and that you care for them. Plus, the word of God is powerful enough to make an impact regardless of how dismissive someone appears.

We shouldn't be looking to pick fights for the sake of being argumentative but more so looking for opportunities to inject God's love into the lives of others.

Instead of hitting someone with the science of the Bible and historical context, try sharing what Jesus has done for you and the world's need for Him. The more you play *Pong*, the better you get, even as it gets harder.

Evangelising can be about practise, with every interaction a chance to have God change a person's eternity.

> *"And he said to them, 'Go into all the world and proclaim the gospel to the whole creation.'"*
>
> —*Mark 16:15*

See also… Matthew 10:17; 2 Timothy 4:2; Luke 6:22, Romans 12:18; Proverbs 15:1; 2 Timothy 2:24

Title: **Holes of Hope**
Game: ***Portal* and *Portal 2***
Themes: **Fallen creation, sin, hope**

THE city is left in ruins, its gate is battered to pieces. The ruined city lies desolate; the entrance to every house is barred.

What a depressing and disturbing start to a video game, waking up in a dystopian world where something has clearly gone wrong between man and the machines.

With little introduction, the player is thrown into the mess, left to piece together what is going on with little but an electronic voice to guide her.

The world is, literally at times, falling away beneath her feet.

It launches what many have regarded as one of the cleverest games to be created. Armed with an Aperture Science Handheld Portal Device (or "portal gun"), it forces the player to think backwards, inside out, reverse, upside down and in opposites.

And that's just to get to places; the ongoing narrative of a world gone to pot adds stress and tension to the plot.

Curiously, those first two lines at the top of this devotion aren't from *Portal 2*. They are from Isaiah 24, describing a world polluted by sin that will endure God's judgment.

Oftentimes it wouldn't be too much of a stretch to believe Isaiah is describing the current world.

There's a lot to be depressed about. Poor government decisions that seem to go against God's plan; trends that are anti-Jesus; arguments over social media; major military hostilities; the rise of new sicknesses; and a seeming lack of cures for lingering ones; the list could go on.

It'd be quite easy to get broken by it all, ground down and trampled with little to look up to.

But Isaiah 24 is not without hope; verses 14-16 has those who still follow God raising their voices, "they shout for joy; from the west they acclaim the Lord's majesty," and exalting the name of the Lord, from the ends of the earth singing is heard: "Glory to the Righteous One."

There is hope in *Portal* as well. The player is equipped with all she needs; a portal gun. But she's got to commit to using it, and then actually use it.

God has equipped us with all we need to not just survive in this decaying world but to make a difference in it and shine for Him.

Two of our main "weapons" are prayer and the Bible but we've got to use them; *really* use them.

Portal doesn't give you a practise arena; you are thrown in and have to learn as you go. There's no practise arena for life. Pick up God's word and pray as you go.

God wants us to do more than just make it through this life. He wants us to live for His glory.

The ultimate hope is, for those accepting of salvation, the thought of eternity with Him; that this world, no matter how it might get us down, is just a temporary point, a stage, a level, before rejoicing with God forever. No portal needed.

> *"For I consider that the sufferings of this present time are not worth comparing with the glory that is to be revealed to us."*
>
> *—Romans 8:18*

See also… Romans 8:20-21; Colossians 3:2; Job 5:7; Isaiah 24

Title: **False Potions and Prophets**
Game: ***Prince of Persia***
Themes: **False teaching**

EVERYTHING seems so fluid in *Prince of Persia*.
It was one of the stand-out features when the original game was released on PC back in 1989.

The prince's running, stopping, turning, jumping, climbing, hanging and sword fighting are all done with grace and agility (even though he's doing it while dressed in a set of white pyjamas).

There is plenty to watch out for; hidden spikes in the floor that appear when approached, falling timber planks disguising secret rooms or passageways, and of course, the very unhelpful chomping metal jaws that inconveniently slice you in half if you mistime the jump.

You can be traveling along quite well, avoiding obstacles and leaping out of danger's way, until you come across a bottle of bubbling fluid.

First-time players wonder what taking a swig from these jars will do. Again, with an effortlessly smooth motion, the prince drinks up.

If the potion is beneficial, his health will be restored; he'll feel refreshed and he'll carry on toward his mission.

If the potion is not as it seems, it will reduce his health, removing a life bar. There are other potions, one of which flips the screen upside down, further hindering his progress.

It's easy to smoothly run through the Christian life, making progress and avoiding the obvious big falls/sins of life filled with savage spikes.

But occasionally we might swig from the wrong bottle of false teaching. Something that looks good, sounds like all the other sermons, messages or articles we've read, yet doesn't quite "taste" right.

Self-help or worldly wisdom can also be a poison potion.

It can set our journey back, maybe even do us harm if we consume too much.

How do we know, though? How do we discern? The Bible says to "test everything" (1 Thessalonians 5:21) and hold fast to what is good.

Ask: How does it measure up to what God's Word says? Is it contradictory to what you know about God already? Is it lifting up Christ or someone's personal view/agenda? If you're still unsure, it's worth checking with an older Christian or someone who has been following Jesus for longer than you have.

Prince of Persia players soon learn to stick with what they know when it comes to potion jars. It's a good attitude for a Christian walk as well. That's holding fast to what is good.

Drink in the Bible first and foremost. Let it reinvigorate you, inspire you and, with the help of the Holy Spirit, drive you on for God.

Learn to "read" the colour of the bubbles rising up from a jar of teaching and whether the teacher really has God's purposes at heart, or if they are wolves in sheep's clothing.

> *"Beware of false prophets, who come to you in sheep's*
> *clothing, but inwardly they are ravenous wolves."*
>
> —*Matthew 7: 15*

See also… Mark 13: 22; 1 Timothy 1: 3-4; 2 Peter 2:1

Title: **The Inner Bout**
Game: *Punch Out!*
Themes: **Battling self, sin nature**

---

*P*UNCH *Out!* seems like an unbalanced undertaking from the start.
There you stand as Little Mac, in the black singlet, shiny red gloves and blue/green shorts, taking on some mammoth fighters in the boxing ring.

The various brawlers, each with a name and personality, line up to take a swing at you. A combination of combinations, plus some ducking, weaving and careful movement sees the diminutive black-singleted man topple these menacing figures such as Piston Hurricane, Kid Quick, Bear Hugger and King Hippo (introduced in the re-branded *Mike Tyson's Punch Out!*).

The player is always the smaller guy and seems up against it, the odds heavily outweighing him.

It's not a hyper realistic boxing game but for all its cartoonishness, *Punch Out!* delivers a sense of the ongoing relentlessness and reflexes needed in the boxing ring.

Imagine if, among all these big, bad and bruising characters, you could fight a clone of yourself? How would that go down?

The Apostle Paul appears to have been a sporting man, referencing various sports of the time like running, wrestling and boxing.

That seems to come through his writing as well, which he uses to relate to his audience such as when talking about the battle we have between our different "selves".

Ephesians 4 talks about "putting off the old self which is being corrupted by deceitful desires" and to "put on the new self, created to be like God in true righteousness and holiness".

It tells of things to get rid of (which, ironically includes "brawling") and things we should be, like kind, compassionate and forgiving.

It's like a boxing match between our old self in sin and our new selves born again in Christ.

It's a lifelong fight, a constant bout done in Christ's strength with the aim of keeping that sin nature in check.

Like some of the patterns within the *Punch Out!* opponents, it's important to see the patterns of our sin nature, be alert to them so as not to succumb to their subtle sucker punch.

Only Jesus living in us can truly keep us that vigilant, that alert to such strategies.

In *Punch Out!*, Little Mac has Doc Louis in his corner as coach. In life, we have Jesus who provides far more than a spit bucket and towel. Draw on Him, give your battles over to Him. The final bell will only sound upon His return. Only then will the fight be over. Ding, ding!

> *"Put off your old self, which belongs to your former manner*
> *of life and is corrupt through deceitful desires."*
>
> *—Ephesians 4: 22*

See also… Ephesians 4: 23; Colossians 2:15; Romans 7:14-15; Galatians 5:17

Title: **Fire When Not Ready**
Game: *R-Type*
Themes: **Prayer**

LIFE can feel like being one small spaceship against thousands of enemies.

That tiny ship, called the R-9 Arrowhead (in the 1987 original that is), flies courageously forward, into the lines of aliens, other ships and weird creatures that emerge.

It soon becomes apparent, within seconds of playing, that continual firing is the key. Like time itself, the side-scrolling nature of the game doesn't let up, always pushing on its left to right trajectory.

It seems the only way through is to fire, fire and fire some more.

Prayer isn't a weapon; it's not used to take down people or destroy enemies (although there are plenty of Old Testament examples of characters praying for victory, and the Psalms contain heaps of pleas to "smite enemies", but let's not get too sidetracked).

Prayer is always available though, like the gun in *R-Type*.

When the hassles, temptations and hurdles of the world roll in, leaning on our trigger button, or praying, is vital.

It seems the only way through is to pray.

Sometimes the firing in *R-Type* is scattered and random, like our prayers can be; desperate, sporadic and intense.

At other times, players will be aware of impending waves of trouble and will begin firing beforehand, anticipating what's coming with a good rhythm and planned flow.

There's no hard and fast way to pray. 1 Thessalonians 5:17 tells us to pray without ceasing, like holding down the trigger (or furiously tapping that control pad).

Now, does pouring out a relentless flow of firepower mean everything will be clear sailing for the R-9 Arrowhead? Not at all. God answers in the right way at the right time, even if that's not our preference.

He wants us to be continually talking to Him. The player doesn't run out of bullets/firepower in *R-Type*; similarly, prayer is a limitless resource.

The player is never left without a gun. Even in the breaks from waves of enemies, players often keep up the firing if not for the practise then for what might be coming, as we just don't know what's around the corner. Romans 12:12 says to continue steadfastly in prayer.

That means keeping it up even in quieter times or when things are sailing along smoothly.

In life, you are never left without being able to pray, even if you can't speak or see or hear or lose all of your senses. The Holy Spirit helps with communicating, a bit like that helpful bot that pops up to take care of those bits that threaten you without noticing.

No shot fired in R-Type is a wasted shot because of the limitless nature of the firepower. No prayer is ever wasted to God, because it's an unlimited well to be tapped and re-tapped and tapped again.

> *"Rejoice always, pray without ceasing, give thanks in all circumstances; for this is the will of God in Christ Jesus for you."*
>
> —*1 Thessalonians 5: 16-18*

See also... 2 Thessalonians 1:11; Colossians 4:2; Romans 12:12; 1 Thessalonians 5:17

Title: A Guiding Voice
Game: *Sega Rally Championship*
Themes: Guidance of the Holy Spirit

"OVER jump" he says. "Easy right… maybe," he then adds. "Caution - hairpin right," comes another direction.

Sega Rally Championship took rally driving games to another level upon its release in 1994.

The free-flowing style of the play (the appeal of drifting on dirt) combined with the rolling graphics featuring actual rally cars (a Lancia Delta HF Integrale, a Toyota Celica GT-Four or a Lancia Stratos HF) makes this game a delight.

The fun is heightened when played against other human players, particularly in an arcade setting within that elaborate cockpit.

One of the parts that make this game memorable is the audio, particularly the speech of the co-pilot.

The vocabulary isn't huge; there are only a handful of comments he makes while tearing around the four tracks but there is a point to them.

They guide the driver to know when to take caution, to slow up or ease into a corner.

The Holy Spirit guides those who have given their lives to Christ.

As fully God within the idea of the Trinity, as are both the Father and Jesus themselves, He is the promised helper Jesus spoke of, saying He would be on earth after the Son returned to heaven.

He dwells within for those who are saved which is certainly a reassuring thought, just as it is for the driver/player knowing the co-pilot has read the map for what's ahead.

The Holy Spirit works by promptings, often through our conscience, speaking through the Bible and from advice of other believers.

We need to be tuned into those murmurings, uneasy feelings or downright plain indicators that God wants us to move in a certain direction or not move, as the case may be.

Generally, it won't be an audible direction by an American accented co-pilot.

In Acts 16, Paul, Silas and Timothy try to travel to Mysia "but the Spirit of Jesus would not allow them to".

Clearly, the Spirit steps in to divert believers to where they should be heading.

Often the co-pilot/Holy Spirit's advice doesn't necessarily make it easier or simpler to navigate but is a reassuring comforter within the race of life.

Of course, you can choose to ignore the Holy Spirit ("grieve it", as the Bible says) but why would a *Sega Rally Championship* player block out the co-pilot? Why block out someone so accessible, designed and given to help you toward the goal of becoming more like Christ, to give Him glory?

Mind the water, take care on the jumps, watch how you handle the drift, but tune in to the Spirit's prompting. He may just save you from crashing out.

"But when the Helper comes, whom I will send to you from the Father, the Spirit of truth, who proceeds from the Father, he will bear witness about me."

—John 15: 26

See also… John 16:13, Acts 16:7-8; 1 Corinthians 2:15; 1 John 2: 26-27

Title: **Staying in Tune with God**
Game: *SingStar*
Themes: **Christian living**

SINGING with friends isn't cool.

At least, it wasn't cool before those *Pitch Perfect* movies.

But even before then, people knew the small exhilaration of belting out a tune into their hair brush while standing in front of the bathroom mirror.

Then, Sony took the hairbrush, replaced it with a microphone and added some genuinely catchy songs.

Hey presto; *SingStar*, an instant gaming hit. Singing with friends was cool.

Sure, karaoke was around for a long time before the PlayStation 2 game came out but this was different.

It was accessible from the living room and had the original soundtracks, not a backing track at all.

The game generated a score as well.

Oh how so many strained vocal chords trying to maintain those sparkles on the blue or red bar in the choruses of Survivor's "*Eye of the Tiger*" or Daniel Bedingfield's "*If You're Not the One*".

Staying in tune does not come naturally for many, particularly when compared to the original artist.

Staying in tune with God (the very first original artist) doesn't either.

The natural sinful nature we're born with constantly pulls us out of time or out of harmony with the Creator.

And it sounds woeful.

Going about things our own way, trying to solve problems as if we know best, indulging in deceitful activities, or bloating our hearts with the pride of self-satisfaction are just some of the ways our life songs get garbled.

God doesn't expect us to be the loudest in the choir, or hit the "Super Star" among the group of gamers every time.

But we've got to aim for the blue line though; the standard that Jesus set.

It means knowing the words, the tune and the timing.

The Christian equivalent in life is knowing the Word (the Bible), being in constant contact with God through prayer and living the way Jesus did.

And practise. You get better at *SingStar* the more you play it. Practise walking in Christ's example and you'll get better at it.

We won't perfect the performance on earth but we can sure aim for perfection. Aiming for anything less is cutting your service short, not giving your all.

Of course, salvation comes through repentance and acceptance of Jesus as Lord and Saviour, not through good singing, or behaviour, but it's *because* we are saved, we have something worth living the right way for. And certainly something worth singing about.

> *"Therefore be imitators of God, as beloved children."*
>
> *—Ephesians 5:1*

See also… Ephesians 5:19; John 13:14-16; 1 Peter 2:20-22

Title: **A Tangle of Lies**
Game: *Snake/Snake II*
Themes: **Lying**

ONE lie isn't such a big deal, is it? Sometimes it's just easier to tell a fib to get out of a situation or avoid a confrontation, right?

The problem with lying is that it's habit forming. One lie, no matter how small, often leads to another, and then to another and then to another.

The trail of lies gets longer and longer, just like the snake in the game *Snake* (or *Snake II*, which is essentially the same game) that appeared on the Nokia 3310 mobile/cell phone.

Played in monochrome green and grey/black, the user plays as a snake that has to eat apples/dots/whatever-they-are on the screen for points.

The trick is though, with each item it eats, the longer the snake gets. This gets challenging as you end up having to avoid your own body which wraps and curls around the screen in the path you've left it.

Should the snake happen to run into itself, it's game over.

Put simply, lying gets tangled.

Curiously, Satan appears as a snake when he addresses Eve in the Garden of Eden, where he lies to her about God's instructions. He's referred to as "the father of lies" which isn't exactly a glowing title to have.

Pretty soon, a habitual liar will have a full time job distorting the truth just to cover up the lies he or she has already told, going from "evil to evil" as the book of Jeremiah puts it.

The snake gets longer the more it swallows until it becomes hard work trying not to get caught.

Eventually though, it will come back to bite itself.

It's easy to think lying isn't as big of a sin as murder or stealing but sin is sin, regardless of its size, and it all creates a barrier between humans and God.

It's possible to lie to a friend or a colleague or a stranger, or even yourself, but you can't lie to God.

1 Samuel 16: 7 says that the Lord does not see as man sees; "for man looks at the outward appearance, but the Lord looks at the heart".

Thankfully, Jesus was willing to die for us to bridge that barrier, to make us right in the sight of God once more.

If we've accepted that forgiveness, we will strive to live to honour him as purely as possible, and that means speaking the truth and living truthfully.

Don't give in to the temptation to lie. It'll only result in a tangled mess with no high score to boast about.

> *"You shall not steal; you shall not deal falsely;*
> *you shall not lie to one another."*

—Leviticus 19: 11

See also… Jeremiah 9: 3-8; Proverbs 19:5; Proverbs 12:22

Title: **Playing the Lazy Card**
Game: *Solitaire*
Themes: **Work, servanthood**

SOMEWHERE, somehow, someone needs to conduct a speculative research project with one question: What could world productivity have been if it hadn't been for *Solitaire*?

Sitting embedded on just about every personal computer since the mid nineties, many wouldn't have realised solitaire was a card game first before it was included as a computer game.

Millions of hours have been poured into shuffling those cards to make the correct order and hoping desperately the next card to appear on the stack would be the required one.

It's interesting to consider why computer manufacturers (we're looking at you, Microsoft) decided to put *Solitaire* in there.

It's a dash of fun, a bit of excitement, a statement that said computers weren't all about serious business.

Receptionists the world over have been, often unfairly, accused of staring at the screen and manoeuvring jacks and spades and aces and clubs to fall into order and get that rewarding "bouncy card effect" when solitaire is achieved.

Then again, receptionists wouldn't be the only ones to have a cheeky play at work. It's a temptation like many things.

Is it the best use of the employees' time and resources to be working with digital cards when real work needs to be done?

God wants us to be vigilant workers; working hard for those who employ us shows our servant attitude, something Jesus exhibited on many occasions.

Of course, your "*Solitaire*" might not be a game at all (although, having picked up this book there's quite a high chance it is a digital game of some description).

Perhaps it's YouTube, Facebook, TikTok, Twitter/X, texting, perusing a magazine/comic/novel, knowingly working at half pace, purposefully wasting stationery, taking extra time during lunch hour, intentionally starting late or finishing early, or whatever.

The point is, we rip off or steal from our employees when we take liberties or take our employment for granted.

After God created Adam, He gave him work to do in the garden. It wasn't a punishment for sin, it was part of the plan.

Work is such an important discipline to embrace from a Biblical perspective.

Let's be mindful not to count cards on the work clock when we should be serving God by working diligently.

"Whatever you do, work heartily, as for the Lord and not for men."

—*Colossians 3:23*

See also... 2 Thessalonians 3: 10-11, Philippians 2:14, Genesis 2:15

Title: **Let Go of Rings and Things**
Game: ***Sonic the Hedgehog***
Themes: **Riches, worldly wealth**

WHEN *Sonic the Hedgehog* first appeared on video game systems for Sega in the 1990s, he was touted as the fastest video game character created.

Often referred to as "the blue blur", Sonic's original games are all about speed and ripping through levels as quickly as possible.

But have you ever played Sonic… slowly? Just ambled your way through it, collecting as many rings as possible and taking in the scenery?

Okay, okay, so the storyline would suggest time is of the essence and it's unlikely Sonic himself would stop for morning tea and to admire a quaint waterfall cascading between checkered brown and orange hills, but there's something to take away from a "Sunday drive" style of playing the creature in the red pointy boots.

When Sonic gets hit, whether he's traveling at full speed or standing still, it's like his world falls apart - rings explode from within him.

Where exactly he is storing all those rings remains a mystery, but that's beside the point.

The player must then make a quick decision (pun intended) - will she/he chase after those rings within reach, or press on, confident the end goal will be better than trying to hold onto something that essentially has no purpose within the game?

What's that? No purpose to those millions of gold rings in *Sonic the Hedgehog* you say? Preposterous!

Well, think it through - they provide points; an extra life if you notch up 100 of them; and they give the option of entering a bonus level - but all of these things are essentially just tooling you up so you can finish the game which involves defeating Dr Robtonik and freeing the animals being turned into robots.

Really, you could play Sonic the Hedgehog without the rings and the game would still work.

It's the end that draws you on to play, not the rings.

For followers of Christ, it's the end that draws us on as well; the promise of life with our Creator after we die. There is something better and bigger beyond these deteriorating bodies, and that's something worth striving for.

There are plenty of "rings" on earth - bright and shiny things that can't be held onto once your last breath is breathed.

Even on earth, money and possessions won't be able to lift you out of all types of trouble.

Don't get caught up with gathering enough "stuff". Look long-term. Look eternal. Look beyond Robotnik even.

You'll soon discover the futility of chasing and collecting rings.

"Do not lay up for yourselves treasures on earth, where moth and rust destroy and where thieves break in and steal, but lay up for yourselves treasures in heaven, where neither moth nor rust destroys and where thieves do not break in and steal. For where your treasure is, there your heart will be also."

—Matthew 6:19-21

See also… 1 Peter 1: 6-9; Hebrews 13: 5; 1 Timothy 6: 17-19

Title: **Practising the Special Moves**
Game: ***Street Fighter II (or Super Street Fighter II, or Street Fighter IV, or ...)***
Themes: **Talents**

CAMMY, Blanka, Dhalsim, Vega, Chun-Li, M. Bison, Ken, Ryu; they were almost like family to so many gamers in the 1990s.

With subsequent sequels/editions of *Street Fighter* now released, they've become familiar to more generations.

The original *Street Fighter II* exploded onto the scene with its multiple characters, flashy artwork and of course, the special moves of the characters.

The special moves were the thing that set *Street Fighter II* above other fighting games at the time.

Each character brings something distinctive to the game, just as every human on earth brings something unique to the world.

The special moves need practise to pull-off correctly. Most consist of a whirl of special button combinations in conjunction with facing the right way, jumping or crouching at the right time and doing all within a matter of seconds when your opponent is exactly where you need him/her/it to be.

It's not easy to make it all happen when needed. The outcome and effects are exciting to watch though.

A fireball or extended fist or pivoting helicopter kick or electrical shock could tip the balance of a match in your favour.

The diversity of characters in the *Street Fighter* series is amazing as well.

From the petite Chun-Li, who looks like a ballet dancer, to the obesely overweight sumo wrestler E. Honda.

God calls our special moves, talents. They are abilities, skills and interests you can utilise to serve Him.

The world would be a bland old place if we were all built the same. Not everyone is designed to run a church kids' club, or preach a sermon, or play guitar for a worship service, or build a new church in a foreign country, or write a series of Christian devotions based on video games.

Your talents might lay in encouraging, teaching, artistic endeavours, practical help, listening, leadership, holding conversations, development, construction, or a thousand other possibilities.

First time players of *Street Fighter II* aren't usually able to launch into the array of moves available to them. It takes time and practise.

The same goes for developing your skillset or gifts to target them for God's purposes.

Take time to learn your special moves; the things that you can pull off to make an impact for God, maybe even affect someone's eternity.

Now that's an outcome beyond winning another credit.

> *"Having gifts that differ according to the grace given to us, let us use them: if prophecy, in proportion to our faith."*

> —*Romans 12: 6*

See also… 1 Corinthians 12: 29-31; 1 Peter 4:10-11; 1 Timothy 4:14

Title: **The Force of Friendship**
Game: *Super Mario Bros.*
Themes: **Friendship**

YOU'VE got to hand it to Luigi; he's a long suffering brother, that's for sure. Okay, so he's been given a few game titles of his own over the years (*Luigi's Mansion*, *New Super Luigi U*, etc) but essentially, he exists in a world named after his brother, Mario.

From the very beginning, back when there wasn't a "super" in their title, there were still the two brothers, running around knocking platforms with their heads and destroying creatures in a sewer-style situation (Atari created an arcade game simply called *Mario Bros*).

Since then, their circle has grown to include, among others, Princess Peach (who has a knack for getting kidnapped), Toadstool and the all-consuming dinosaur, Yoshi.

The group now re-appears in all sorts of Mario incarnations, from driving go-karts to competitive party games.

The circle of friends helps Mario along the way. They provide gifts, advice, guidance and in some cases, solutions to problems that can't be solved alone.

The theme of friendship seems to extend into how the game is physically played as well, with *New Super Mario Bros.* and *Super Mario Wonder* allowing multiple players to jump around on screen at one time.

Video games have gone beyond a single person sitting in a bedroom, curtains drawn with the glowing screen the only light in the room.

They have become a social entertainment form. Do you play games with your friends, or brothers or sisters, your parents perhaps? Playing with someone can add an extra element of fun.

We can underestimate the need for friends and the importance of being a friend. Like Mario, our circle of chums can help us through situations, provide advice, listen to our struggles and even provide gifts.

Jesus had a circle of friends around Him. None of them were mushrooms or wore a way-out green and blue uniform (as far as we know) but they were a trusted group Jesus found comfort in.

They didn't always live up to the plan though. Just before Jesus was about to be arrested and taken away for trial, eventually leading Him to die on the cross, He asked His friends to stay with Him and pray. They fell asleep; not once, but three times. Their hearts were in the right place but they couldn't deliver.

Appreciate your friends but remember that they are human, so sometimes they'll mess up. This goes for online friends as well, those in your clan or guild or team for online play.

You're human too. Chances are you'll let down a friend, so it's nice to think your relationship will survive these times. Jesus says to forgive each other, like He forgave you. (Ephesians 4:32)

Perhaps we need to think of our friendships as opportunities to give, rather than expectations of what we *should* receive; a reflection of the divine.

The next time you're with your friends, whether it's at school, work, sport, a party, a shared gaming experience, youth group, church, battling Koopa Troopers or whatever, ask yourself: Are you being the best friend you can be?

"This is my commandment, that you love one another as I have loved you,"

—John 15: 12

See also… John 15: 13-14; Ephesians 4:32; Ecclesiastes 4:9-12

Title: **Just One More**
Game: *Tetris*
Themes: **Covetousness, provision**

THAT one long block. It's coming soon, isn't it? You just need it to fill that gap down the side.

You can keep shuffling, keep building up the other side, but you really, really need that long, straight block.

And just when you think it's about to drop, you get that annoying z-shaped monstrosity which throws everything out of whack.

It doesn't fit; it creates a gap in the line and suddenly things are piling up all over the place.

Tetris could be the most beloved form of frustration in the world. Few games capture puzzle-loving minds like this classic.

If you've ever been in the situation above, waiting for that long, straight block, you're not alone.

It often seems like we're waiting for that one particular block to complete our career or hobby goal checklist.

We wait for one more thing in life to complete us, to make the "lines", to make us complete.

If we can just get that promotion; get put in that sporting position; are able to afford that pair of shoes; find a shortcut in these streets, then everything will click together nicely.

Perhaps it's a girl/boy you're chasing, or waiting to reach a particular age, or own a certain car, or obtain the next generation console or upgrade the PC?

Are you leading a life of "if only I get…" I'll be complete?

But rarely, in *Tetris* as in life, does another piece completely satisfy. Why is that?

Stacking up "things" always creates another gap. It's human nature to cling, want, lust for the next item or checkpoint.

But what happens when we get that z-shaped block falling down upon us, something that doesn't fit into our plans?

Many stop to ask why God has sent the z-shaped block.

Tetris players know that z-shaped blocks, like all of them, are important and serve a purpose.

We need to realise God has provided for us before - sent that long brick when needed - but it may not be in our timing.

It might be a few lines higher than we wanted but it still comes, and it's for the best.

Trust that God has all the bricks in view and knows what blessings are good for us.

> *"Many are the plans in the mind of a man, but it is*
> *the purpose of the Lord that will stand."*
>
> —*Proverbs 19: 21*

See also… Proverbs 16:9; Matthew 6: 25-34

Title: **Learning to Use the Sword**
Game: ***The Legend of Zelda***
Themes: **God's Word**

SHIELDS and swords and boots and maps and gold and bows and bombs and hookshots and boomerangs and Ocarinas; that Link fellow must have some deep pockets.

Legend of Zelda fans know these games are about exploration and collecting stuff. Sometimes a lot of stuff. The same basic plan exists in all the Zelda titles be it on Game Boy, NES, Nintendo 64, GameCube, Wii, Wii U or Switch; there is a land to explore and a mission to complete.

The collected items aren't just for decoration though. It's highly unlikely Link was just going to grab Majora's Mask to take home and put above the fireplace to have as a talking point when friends come round. There's a purpose to each thing. You get something in order to complete a task, save someone or get another item. Now take that Bible of yours from out the drawer and think of it like a Zelda game. Yes, yes, there are less chickens in the Bible than are scattered throughout the land of Hyrule, but go ahead. Take that Bible and explore it. Go for a wander through its pages, searching, hunting and picking up treasures along the way.

There's a distinct advantage the Bible has over Zelda. Parts of Link's map (in the original games at least) remain locked until you open up a certain area or solve a certain riddle; not so for the Bible.

It's "open all access". You can flick from Revelation to Exodus; 2 Peter to Lamentations via Malachi if you like, and there's nothing to stop you.

As you read you will find that by collecting "items" (ie. pieces of information from God, even bits of history) you will be able to better understand and perhaps "unlock" other areas.

It's also a life-changing thing to do. The Word of God is a powerful thing and works on our minds and souls. We might not always see the effects straight away but long-term, the maturing effect of God's word will come into play, as it will when faced with a difficult situation

You'll note the encouragement at the start was to physically pull the Bible from a drawer. You may wonder, why don't I just read it on my phone or online?

Good point; go ahead, there's nothing wrong with that. And yep, the Bible is available in this day and age in more forms than it ever has been.

There is a sense of adventure though about actually opening a book. Perhaps it helps you better learn the books of the Bible by having to go to the contents and turn the actual pages instead of just typing the book and verses into a search engine.

Still, use whatever works for you. Grab it, explore it, sift through it, take some treasures away and solve some problems with it.

You don't even have to save the game. (Although a bookmark might be handy if you want to come back to something.)

"For the word of God is living and active, sharper than any two-edged sword, piercing to the division of soul and of spirit, of joints and of marrow, and discerning the thoughts and intentions of the heart."

—Hebrews 4:12

See also… Ephesians 6: 16-17; Psalm 119: 105; Joshua 1: 8; 2 Timothy 3: 16-17

Title: Encouragement Like a Pirate
Game: *The Secret of Monkey Island*
Themes: Encouragement

IN the mid nineties, groups of friends pored over the problems that *The Secret of Monkey Island*, a point-and-click adventure, delivered.

The genre seemed to die a death towards the end of that decade.

For those who haven't played it, gameplay consists of solving problems through collecting and using items at the right moments, or having the right interactions with other characters.

The Secret of Monkey Island did something for its time that other games were not doing; it delivered humour.

Yep, we were actually laughing at a video game.

It adds an extra element of fun to playing it, alongside the challenge of finding out why there is a pulley inside a rubber chicken and what is the future use for a pair of wax lips.

The storyline has you take up the role of want-to-be pirate Guybrush Threepwood, learning the ropes of pirating.

Not only do you have to have your wits about you when it comes to solving problems, you have to know what to say at precisely the right time.

This is how sword fights are done in the game. It isn't so much about your ability with the blade but more about what insult you manage to hurl at your opponent. Again, it's part of the humour of the game. So for instance, if someone says to you: "You fight like a dairy farmer", then you're presented with a list of possible responses.

It is up to you to select the right one, which in this case is the witty retort: "How appropriate - you fight like a cow."

Dialogue at its best, as you can see.

God doesn't want us hurling insults at each other but the lesson here is about the timing of comments.

The Bible says there is a season for everything; laughing, crying, rejoicing, mourning (Ecclesiastes 3). A few carefully chosen words can really pick a person up from an otherwise horrendous day or situation.

Appropriate words, whether they are verbal, handwritten, in a text, voice message or e-mail, may just be the best gift you give someone at that moment.

It pays to consult with God before going in with your mouth blazing. In *The Secret of Monkey Island*, it isn't always the long-winded comeback that is the winner.

Sometimes, less is more. A word of encouragement or sympathy can be God working through you to show His care for that person, or even prove His existence.

When the opportunity comes to interact with a person (no swords of course), check with God before engaging your mouth; the words you use could say more than you think.

> *"To make an apt answer is a joy to a man, and*
> *a word in season, how good it is!"*
>
> *—Proverbs 15:23*

See also… Proverbs 25:11; Isaiah 50:4; 1 Thessalonians 5:11

Title: Blessings Beyond Pink Flamingos
Game: *The Sims*
Themes: God's provision

THE swimming pool in the backyard with the jacuzzi to the side and the light-up dance-floor on the other.

Who wouldn't be happy with all this?

Life simulation doesn't get much more detailed than *The Sims*. From the colour of a person's jeans through to the tiles in their kitchen, you can select and adjust nearly all aspects of the lives of these digital beings.

At the basis of the gameplay is existence, something that really isn't too hard to achieve. Afterall, you don't even have to give birth to them really; they just appear there.

It's the add-ons and items that make the game really fun. There's always another item to get, or a new look to strive for.

There is a great attraction in being in control of a group of people and providing for them. We love to give them more than the basics, we love to give blessings so they know they are loved.

God works on a much larger scale than decorative coffee tables and pink flamingos for the garden.

He knows what we need and when we need it. Now, it may not always be what we want and in our timing but you've got to have faith in His "playing strategy".

He knows what we are thinking and doesn't need speech-bubbles above our heads with symbols and logos to show what we feel and desire.

God is the ultimate multi-tasker. It's like He is caring for each of us "Sims" individually, as if we are the only players in the game but knowing that we need each other.

His focus is as much on us as individuals as it is on the entire nation, state, country and planet.

That's a concept that might be hard to get our finite minds around.

The common earthly trap to fall into is to look at the Sims next door and wonder why they have the expensive trimmings, the full regal living set and the virtuoso violin; why would God bless them more than me?

The answer may be that God knows how much you need. People who have a lot always seem to want more; it's a never ending cycle, so in a way, having less reduces stress and temptation.

Adding to that then, think about how boring life would be if we all had the same?

And even those with all the "stuff" still have to be fed and cared for.

There is an old saying: "The more you have, the more you have to lose." It could all go in an instant; a fire, flood, cyclone, tornado, mudslide and it's all turned to rubbish.

The trick, if you need to call it that, is to count the blessings you do have, and praise God for them.

God gives us more than enough to exist on this planet, and more than we deserve to be perfectly honest.

Don't focus on wanting pink flamingos in the front yard; give thanks for the front yard in the first place.

> *"And my God will supply every need of yours according to his riches in glory in Christ Jesus."*
>
> —*Philippians 4:19*

See also… Psalm 23; Luke 12: 22-31

Title: Discovering Real Beauty
Game: *Tomb Raider*
Themes: Inner beauty

POOR old Lara Croft.

Misjudged from her very first outing as primarily a pretty face, even if that face was rather pixelated on the 1996 PlayStation.

Here is a woman who is every part Indiana Jones' equal, albeit to a different generation.

She can perform miraculous backflips from standing still, haul herself up from sheer cliff faces, hold her breath for several minutes while swimming through tight crevices, push massive stone blocks and dodge darts shot from walls.

Ms Croft can do all this of course while solving ancient puzzles and navigating dark and other worldly labyrinths.

She's not afraid to call on those twin Heckler & Koch USP Match pistols famously strapped to her thighs either, not hesitating to dispose of blood-sucking bats, bears, crocodiles, mutants, wolves, lions, velociraptors, the odd person and of course, a towering Tyrannosaurus Rex that comes out to play.

But for all these abilities and qualities, it is so often Lara Croft's looks which stick in the memory for most gamers of that era. She was a revelation in gaming, being a rough and tumble female lead.

The long French braid which swishes as she runs, those very nineties round sunglasses, the tanktop, the high-cut khaki shorts and, well, her unrealistic "proportions", shall we say.

She became, and remains, the dream girl of many adolescent male video gamers.

People are often summed up by how they look. If they are untidy and have unusual features, it's easy to dismiss them as untalented, unskilled and uneducated.

Conversely, if they are a stunning, cave adventuring beauty, it's easy to assume they have it all together and not a care in the world.

God looks beyond the skin though (1 Samuel 16:7) to the heart. He knows the attitudes and abilities of people despite their outer appearance.

In fact, the Bible says God chose what is low and despised in the world to do His work and get things done.

We have to replicate that attitude, shelving our judgment of people based on their initial looks, speech and even odour.

God has given gifts to each of those willing to serve Him.

When trying to get through a jungle or dank rocky cavern, it'll be Lara's climbing, leaping, endurance and flexibility that will help; not her model good-looks and styling.

Appreciate everyone you come in contact with as one of God's children, knowing their skills and talents may lie deeper within, like a gleaming artifact waiting to be discovered.

"But the Lord said to Samuel, "Do not look on his appearance or on the height of his stature, because I have rejected him. For the Lord sees not as man sees: man looks on the outward appearance, but the Lord looks on the heart."

—1 Samuel 16:7

See also… Matthew 7: 1-3, Matthew 23: 26-28, 1 Peter 3:3-4, Proverbs 31:30

Title: **Get Off the Couch**
Game: ***Wii Sports***
Themes: **Serving**

WHEN it first came out and the buzz around the Nintendo Wii was still new, families were treating *Wii Sports* like a bowling simulator more than a game.

It was like having a real-life bowling alley in your lounge room, without the smell of hot chips/fries and the sound of a 16-year-old DJ being told to play songs from before he was born.

Players rose from the couch when it was their turn, strapped on the all-important wrist band attached to the Wii remote and prepared to bowl.

It was an all-of-body experience with some players even beginning with a small jog on the spot as if approaching the lane, then finishing with a follow-through motion as the ball was launched.

This was all followed by a triumphant shout and a punching of the air in celebration if the pins scattered.

It was a familiar scene across the world in family homes, retirement villages, university dorms and bachelor pads.

As time wore on though, and human laziness kicked in, people found they didn't exactly need to put their whole bodies behind their deliveries.

In fact, some became so reckless they didn't even bother putting on the remote safety strap anymore (gasp!). It became apparent there was no need to even stand up.

Pretty soon, experienced Wii bowlers were barely moving from their sprawled out position of comfort, flicking their wrists and still notching up strikes and spares.

If you've ever played Wii bowling with others and been the only one that jumped to your feet while the others slothed about, you'll know how sapping that is. It drains the atmosphere out of the game.

New Christians and those involved with a new ministry or a new church activity are often on their feet, ready to get involved, do whatever it takes and put in the extra effort.

Then the reality of routine kicks in. What was once a 110% attitude in serving gets simplified and numbed down to just going through the motions.

Sure, the Sunday school class is being delivered or the worship leading is being done or the morning devotions are being plodded through but the zest and sparkle seem to have waned.

It happens to everyone. It's the simple grind of ministry. That doesn't make it right though.

It pays to check our status; are we simply going through the motions of outreach and ministry? Are we ambling our way through our daily walk with God? Are we plonked on the couch, just flicking our wrists when we should be on our feet, ready to serve?

As a member of Christ's body, your attitude, enthusiasm and approach will affect those around you.

The last thing you want to do is hinder someone who is "strapped in" and ready to get active for God.

Take time to re-think, re-assess and re-acquaint yourself with how God wants you to serve.

And don't be afraid to follow through.

"For we are not, like so many, peddlers of God's word, but as men of sincerity, as commissioned by God, in the sight of God we speak in Christ."

—*2 Corinthians 2: 17*

See also… 2 Corinthians 2:15; Revelation 2: 2- 5; Colossians 3:23-24

Title: A Protective Suit
Game: Wonder Boy III: The Dragon's Trap
Themes: Defensive living

ALL of a sudden, Tom-Tom (Wonder Boy) went from a blonde-haired, fruit-guzzling, hatchet-throwing, sometimes-skateboard-riding jungle lad, to a knight, capable of mowing down enemies with swords and using magic.

So was the progress of the *Wonder Boy* series from the original arcade and Sega Master System title through to *Wonder Boy in Monster Land*, *Wonder Boy III: The Dragon's Trap*, *Wonder Boy in Monster World* and *Monster World IV*.

But it's the third entry which captured many hearts and minds as the now green-haired Wonder Boy (perhaps it's not the original Tom-Tom at all?) gets turned into various creatures (ie. Lizard-Man, Mouse-Man, Piranha-Man, Lion-Man and Hawk-Man) as he fights to become human again.

Regardless of his form, Wonder Boy can buy/find/receive different swords, shields and armour.

There are many games which allow the player to change up armour and swords, each with different abilities and strengths. The Bible gives its own set of armour, outlined in Ephesians 6. Here it lists six items:

1) Belt of truth;
2) Breastplate of righteousness;
3) Shoes of the preparation of the gospel of peace;
4) Shield of faith;
5) Helmet of salvation;
6) Sword of the Spirit, the Word of God.

They almost sound like they could exist within a video game but they are much more than that.

The armour that Wonder Boy puts on isn't just to look good; it serves a purpose and is often needed to complete a specific task.

The "armour of God" is not just for looks either. It serves a purpose. Each item helps the wearer so he or she "may be able to stand against the wiles of the devil".

There's a defensive tone here, to protect the wearer. It's not about attacking but bracing for the inevitable fight the devil will put up as he goes about "like a roaring lion, seeking whom he may devour" (1 Peter 5:8).

Note that the armour should be worn as a whole; it's a set, designed for a Christian to stay strong against so many temptations which could cause us to stumble.

Read Ephesians 6 and explore what each item means in full.

Wonder Boy fights off skeletons (some with top hats), crabs, cogs, fish, clouds (some with sunglasses), snakes and frogs by relying on his armour, shield and sword.

We too can tackle the adventure of each new day, despite the broad range of challenges thrown at us when we fully trust in God's power through the armour He has given us made up of truth, righteousness, peace, faith and salvation.

> *"Put on the whole armor of God, that you may be able to stand against the wiles of the devil."*
>
> *—Ephesians 6 : 11*

See also… Isaiah 59:17; 1 Peter 5:8; Psalm 7:10

www.ingramcontent.com/pod-product-compliance
Lightning Source LLC
LaVergne TN
LVHW051506070426
835507LV00022B/2947